Places to go and **Things to do**
Out and About
in the North Country

Kendall Taylor

Second Edition

Designed by Sheila Rae Neal

Copyright information:
Second edition 2021
First edition 2005

Published by:
North Country Children's Museum

Potsdam, New York 13676
USA

ISBN: 978-1-7923-5343-7
Printed by Coughlin Press, Watertown and Lowville, New York

All rights reserved. No part of this publication may be reproduced except for purpose of review without the written permission of the publisher or author.

©Kendall Taylor

Cover photo: Sheila Rae Neal

Introduction

The North Country is known for its beautiful scenery, great hiking trails and fabulous fishing. But it also has incredible museums, amusement parks and ski slopes. You simply have to know where to go. If you need help answering the question, "what can we do today?", and are looking for interesting and fun things to do in the North Country, this guide is for you. For parents with kids of all ages, it offers comprehensive information on hundreds of things to do in the North Country and beyond. Filled with suggestions about where to bike, camp, fish and canoe, it's packed with hours of fun-filled activities from short outings to day trips in one handy easy guide. Covering everything from paddling down the Grasse River to scuba diving in the St. Lawrence, snowshoeing in South Colton or picking apples at local orchards, it's loaded with off the beaten track experiences and inside scoops on the area's most interesting attractions. Arranged alphabetically so you can randomly search and including an index, it's your ticket to family fun.

Stock the car with some snacks, a change of clothes, snow and rain gear, then go! Take along some bug spray in summer and an extra sweater in winter along with your camera or smart phone. Keep in mind this guide was completed during the 2020 COVID Pandemic, so call ahead to see if opening hours have changed.

Acknowledgements

This guide was a project of the North Country Children's Museum completed with the work of volunteers and staff members who did the research and writing, took photographs, edited and assisted with proofreading.

Our appreciation to the following for assistance with publication costs:
- The Adirondack Foundation, Adirondack for Kids Fund
- Price Chopper, Golub Foundation
- From the Heart Cabinetry
- St. Lawrence County Chamber of Commerce
- Pete and Kathy Wyckoff
- Jane Lammers
- Nikki Coates and Associates
- Nancy and Michael Griffin
- Clarkson University
- Big Spoon Kitchen
- Jake's on the Water
- Wendy and Allan Williams
- Kinney Drugs, a KPH Healthcare Services, Inc. Company

We are also grateful to the following for assistance with editorial content and photos:
- Sharon Vegh Williams
- Friends of Higley Flow
- Jonnie Claeys and Brooke Rouse of the St. Lawrence County Chamber of Commerce
- Tom Holsen
- North Country This Week
- Potsdam Recreation Department

And special thanks to staff members Dan Bellinger, Emilia Gatti and Rachael Clements for line edits, and Board Member Nancy Griffin for her tireless efforts fundraising for this project.

Contents

Introduction	3	Hockey	57
Acknowledgements	4	Horseback Riding	58
Amusement Parks and Playgrounds	6	Ice Fishing	59
		Ice Skating	60
Apple Orchards	8	Islands	61
Art Galleries	11	Libraries	63
Balloon Rides	12	Lighthouses	65
Beaches	12	Maple Syrup Tours	66
Bike Shops	13	Marinas	67
Biking	13	Miniature Golf	70
Bird Watching	15	Mountain Biking	71
Boat Rentals	18	Movie Theaters	71
Boat Tours	20	Museums	72
Bowling Alleys	24	Nature Trails	77
Canoeing, Kayaking, and Rowing	26	Plane Rides	79
		Private Campgrounds	80
Calendars of Events	28	Public Concerts	82
Cider Mills	28	Rafting Trips	83
Cross-Country (Nordic) Ski Trails	29	Road Biking	83
		Scuba Diving	84
Disc Golf	31	Shipwrecks	85
Downhill Skiing	32	Sledding	86
Drive-in Movies	34	Snowmobiling	86
Driving Tours	35	Snowshoeing	88
Fairs, Festivals, and Events	36	Special Tours	89
		Speedboat Rides	91
Fishing	47	State Campgrounds	92
Fishing Licenses	49	State Parks	93
Fishing Guides	51	Stock Car Races	97
Forts	52	Swimming Pools	98
Golfing	53	Train Trips	99
Guide Services	55	Waterfalls	100
Hayrides, Sleigh Rides, and Dog Sled Rides	55	Wildlife Refuges	101
		Zoos	102
Hiking	56	Just Over The Border	103

Amusement Parks and Playgrounds

Miniature golf, bowling, batting cages, Go-Karts and bumper cars are activities families can check out for fun and exercise. Miniature golfing is also available at Black Lake Mini Golf in Black Lake, TimeQuest Mini Golf in Massena, SwingTime Mini Golf in Potsdam, and River Adventure Golf in Clayton.

Besides swimming in the scenic lakes and rivers scattered throughout the North Country, families can cool off at the Ogdensburg Municipal Pool, Riverside Drive and Isabella, Ogdensburg. The in-ground facility overlooks the St. Lawrence River and includes a full-sized pool with diving boards and a separate kiddie wading pool.

Most communities have well-maintained playgrounds. Some of the features are elaborate wooden structures where kids can stretch their muscles and imaginations! Large playgrounds can be found in Canton, Potsdam, Ogdensburg, DeKalb and other towns. Local schools also have playgrounds that can be used after school hours and in the summer.

The St. Lawrence Centre Sports Complex in Massena offers a year-round safe and fun environment for a wide array of activities such as recreational or professional sports teams, fitness programs, kids' parties, banquets, indoor driving range, miniature golf, and an arcade. If you like skating, most communities have ice arenas for family skating. Some skating areas to check out are the Malone Civic Center in Malone, Pine Street Arena in Potsdam and the Canton Pavilion Ice Rink in Canton to name a few. Outdoor tennis courts are also available in many communities.

Places where families can bike, hike, rollerblade, walk and jog are located throughout St. Lawrence, Franklin, and Jefferson County. One popular spot is a 3.3 mile-paved path in Canton that's adjacent to the Partridge Run Golf. You will find a sandbox playground just off the path for your children to enjoy.

AMUSEMENT PARKS

Alex Bay 500 Go-Karts & Wilderness Falls Mini-Golf
43772 Route 12, Alexandria Bay
(315) 482-2021
www.alexbay500.com
Try out the 1-mile long fully lit track. Children must be 10 years or older and 54" tall to ride alone or they can be accompanied by a paying adult. You can also enjoy the Mini-Golf course and Amusement Arcade for a fun-filled family day.

Sylvan Beach Amusement Park
112 Bridge Street, Sylvan Beach
(315) 762-5212
www.sylvanbeachamusementpark.com
Take your family to this small retro fun park that offers family rides, bumper cars/boats, mini-golf, carousel and carnival treats. It is about a 2 hour and 45 minute drive from Potsdam.

Thunder Island
21 Wilcox Road, Fulton
(315) 598-8016
www.thunder-island.com
Your whole family will enjoy a day at Thunder Island. You and your children will shoot down waterslides, experience a zip line, and race go-karts for a day to remember. They also have toddler attractions and an arcade. The trip takes about 2.5 hours from Potsdam.

Water Safari Resort
3183 NY-28, Old Forge
(315) 369-6145
www.watersafari.com
If you like adventure parks, your family will enjoy over 50 rides in and out of the water, from speed slides and kiddie pools to bumper cars and a Ferris wheel. There is something for all ages. Some restrictions apply so check out the website. The resort is about 2.5 hours from Potsdam.

WonderWorks Destiny
9090 Destiny, Syracuse
(315) 598-8016
www.wonderworksonline.com
Located at Destiny USA, Mall, this attraction has 100+ hands-on science exhibits, laser tag, rope course and a 6D motion ride. The little ones can do Sky Tykes, a rope course for small children. While there, grab lunch at the many restaurants or walk the mall for some great shopping. This is about a 2.5-hour trip from Potsdam.

PLAYGROUNDS
Adirondack Carousel/Playground
2 Depot Street, Saranac Lake
(518) 891-9521
www.adirondackcarousel.org
The Adirondack Carousel was an idea of Karen Loffler who formed a group of volunteers and recruited area woodcarvers and sponsors to make this a reality. This was "built with community hands" and is truly unique. The doors opened in 2012, featuring a 3,600 square foot pavilion that includes gallery, workshop and classroom space. Outside is a playground and 24 handcrafted wildlife animals, 18 of which are always on display. A wheelchair accessible chariot is also available. Your family will truly enjoy this much visited place.

Kids Kingdom Playground Morrissette Park
100 Riverside Avenue, Ogdensburg
www.northcountryfamily.com/ogdensburg-parks-and-playgrounds
Explore a day at the park, the skate park, or the large wooden fort-style playground surrounded by a fence overlooking the water. The wooden fort is a great play space with sneaky corridors, stairs, platforms, slides, and swings including one for children with physical limitations. Take your family to enjoy the park and great scenery for a fun day.

Kay's Play Space in Ives Park (in memory of Kay Trithart)
3 Riverside Drive, Potsdam
See Ives Park Playscape on Facebook or www.facebook.com/IvesParkPlayscape
This playground was built in 2018 in downtown Potsdam at Ives Park overlooking the Racquette River. It features a natural playground area and there are benches and an adult swing to enjoy the views of the river.

Apple Orchards

BROOKDALE ORCHARD
1997 Route 49, Winthrop
(315) 389-5840
www.facebook.com/Brookdale-Orchard
The Brookdale Orchard was established in 1977 with a u-pick apple orchard offering Honeycrisp, McIntosh, and Cortland apples. If you enjoy picking your own apples, this is a place to visit.

CANTON APPLES U-PICK
Corner of County Route 25 and Barnes Road, Canton
(315) 212-0950
www.cantonapples.com
Founded in 2011, the farm's u-pick orchard boasts 155 trees. Popular varieties include Liberty, MacFree, Honeycrips, Sweet Sixteen, McIntosh, and more. Available are apples u-pick or pre-picked and they also sell other orchard's apples in order to offer a larger variety for their customers. You won't be disappointed. There's ample off-road parking, as well as public restrooms.

CHAZY ORCHARD
9486 Route 9, Chazy
(518) 846-7171
www.chazy.com
The Chazy Orchard known for being the largest McIntosh Apple Orchard was originally established in the 1920's and has expanded to about 120,000 trees plus 20,000 seedlings. The orchard annually produces nearly 300,000 bushels of a variety of apples. Stop in and visit the Farm Market to purchase your apples, unique gifts, baked goods, maple syrup, jams, cider, honey, and much more.

FOBARE'S FRUITS
180 Johnson Road, Rensselaer Falls
(315) 344-1207 or (315) 528-0052
www.fobaresfruits.com This family owned and operated farm and u-pick orchard offers 25 varieties, including Autumn Crisp, Jonagold, and Red Delicious apples. You can also enjoy the experience of u-pick raspberries and grapes. At the Apple Barn Gift Shop, you can enjoy quality products that include fruits, cider jams, local honey, pickles, mixes, cheeses, a full line of maple syrup products, and other unique country food. Make sure you try the hot apple cider donuts, pies, apple crisp, fresh bread, and their famous apple cinnamon rolls that are made daily. The Apple Barn also carries a variety of unique gifts. For family fun, let your little ones loose on "Fort Applewood," a fun-filled playground which features bouncy pillows, covered wagons, a corn maze, tire fort, pumpkin patch, and more! There is a fee for Fort Applewood. No pets, food, or drink allowed.

GOODWIN'S ORCHARD
37 Needham Road, Potsdam
(315) 265-6161
www.facebook.com/goodwinsorchard
Visit this family owned and operated apple orchard planted on six acres with over twelve varieties of New York's favorite apples. The orchard is open to the public for the fun experience of u-pick, all season long. Also, grown and available at a roadside stand are pumpkins, gourds, squash and Indian corn. Wagon rides are offered by request.

KANEB ORCHARD
182 Highland Road, Massena
(315) 769-2880
www.kaneborchards.com
The Kaneb Orchard offers fresh fruit and more than 30 varieties of apples picked daily. Their on-site cider mill produces all-natural fresh pressed apple cider, and homemade baked goods like cider donuts, apple crumb cakes and cranberry walnut cookies. Stop in for a bag of your favorite apples or a wholesome and healthy snack. Sold by 112-peck, 112-bushel.

OWL'S LANDING
7411 West Road, Lowville
(315) 376-2268
www.owlslandingfarm.com

The Owls Landing farm has been in existence for over 40 years. They use organic practices for their crops producing a very nutritious and great tasting product. The farm grows over 20 different varieties of apples that ripen from late July through late October. Other offerings you might want to try is their farm grown honey and maple syrup.

PARISHVILLE CENTER APPLE ORCHARD
765 State Route 72, Potsdam
(315) 212-7057
www.facebook.com/ParishvilleCenterOrchardNY

You don't have to travel far for great apples, fruits, and vegetables. Visit this North Country u-pick orchard and roadside stand that has expanded to over 400 trees. Varieties include Honeycrisp, Liberty, Cortland, Empire, Mac, Gala, and Zestar.

PRAIRIE'S ORCHARD
111 County Route 24, Malone
(518) 483-3760
www.facebook.com/prairiesorchard

Visit this family owned and operated since 2014 upstate u-pick apple and farm stand orchard that has seven varieties of apples, soon to be ten varieties, and approximately 875 trees. Highly recommended is a tour of the orchard. Apples are on display with the different colors, sizes, and tastes that can be found among the rows of trees and varieties. Other offerings are a variety of products including maple syrup/cream, honey, soap, and other seasonal goodies. Pick your own on weekends.

WHEN CAN YOU PICK APPLES?
Early September through October is the best time to pick apples for most of the U.S. and Canada. Of course, some varieties of apples will ripen before others, and it will depend on when they were planted. Each orchard will be on their own schedule. Be sure to check what is available before you visit.

New York State is the second-largest apple producing state in the country. There are many varieties of apples grown in New York: Empire, Fortune, Jonagold, Jonamac, Paula Red, Rubyfrost, and Snapdragon.

Art Galleries

ADIRONDACK ARTISTS GUILD GALLERY
52 Main Street, Saranac Lake (518) 891-2615
www.AdirondackArtistsGuild.com guild@adirondackartistsguild.com
Co-op gallery featuring the work of 15 regional artists
Summer: open every day Mon-Sat 10-5; Thurs til 7; Sun 11-3.
Winter: closed Monday

ART AT THE PINK HOUSE
25 Woodruff Street, Saranac Lake (518) 524-0533
pinkhousegallery@gmail.com
Art gallery and studio specializing in fiber and mixed media art.
Open by chance or appointment.

RICHARD F. BRUSH GALLERY
St. Lawrence University, Canton (315) 229-5174
www.stlawu.edu/gallery
Programs of rotating exhibitions during the academic year. Oversees the university's permanent collection – strengths in 20th century American photographs, prints, portfolios and artists books.

CAPE AIR GALLERY
5 Broadway, Saranac Lake
www.SaranacLakeArtsworks.com info@saranaclakeartworks.com
In cooperation with ArtWorks, Cape Air provides a spacious office and window exhibition venue for artists.
Open Daily

CASAGRAIN GALLERY
68 Park Street, Tupper Lake (518) 359-2595
casagraingallery@outlook.com
Fine art gallery showing wildlife and Adirondack scenes by Gary Casagrain.
Call for hours of operation.

DOWNTOWN ARTIST CELLAR
410 East Main Street, Malone (518) 651-5172
downtownartistcellar@icloud.com
Art studio and gallery.
Open Thurs-Sat 10-4 and by appointment

ROLAND GIBSON GALLERY
SUNY Potsdam (315) 267-2345 www.potsdam.edu.gibson
Collections and exhibitions of 20th century and contemporary art.

IVA SMITH MEMORIAL GALLERY OF FINE ART
627 State Hwy 37, Hammond (315) 324-7467 www.ivasmithgallery.com
Housed in a restored 19th century barn and devoted to the visionary artwork of R. Paul Saphier, the gallery also hosts musical concerts, ukulele classes, art workshops and several barn quilts.
Open seasonally.

MARK KURTZ PHOTOGRAPHY
52 Main Street, 2nd floor, Saranac Lake (518) 891-2431
mark@markkurtzphogography.com
Fine art photography gallery

THE MYERS FINE ARTS BUILDING
SUNY Plattsburgh (518) 564-2000 **www.plattsburgh.edu**
A year-round schedule of changing exhibitions. Home of the Nina Winkel Sculpture Court as well as the most complete and balanced Rockwell Kent Collection in the U.S.

NORTHWIND FINE ARTS GALLERY
11 Woodruff Street, Saranac Lake (518) 354-1875
northwindfindarts@gmail.com Original artworks by Adirondack artists in all media, jewelry and photography.
Open Jan-April: Wed-Sun 11-5; May-Dec: Mon, Wed, Thur, Fri 11-5, Sat 11-6, Sun 11-4 (closed Tues)

ST. LAWRENCE COUNTY ARTS COUNCIL
Village of Potsdam Civic Center, 2 Park Street, Potsdam (315) 265-6868
www.slcartscouncil.org Several artist exhibits annually.
Currently exhibits at Potsdam Town Hall, 41 Elm Street

SMALL FORTUNE STUDIO
76 Main Street, Saranac Lake (518) 891-1139
smallfortunestudio@gmail.com
Experience works in progress and view framed oils and watercolors.
Open Tue-Sat 10-3

TAUNY – TRADITIONAL ARTS IN UPSTATE NEW YORK
53 Main Street, Canton (315) 386-4289 **www.tauny.org** info@tauny.org
Produces three or four temporary exhibits each year.
Open Mon-Fri 10-5, Sat 10-4

THOUSAND ISLANDS ART CENTER
314 John Street, Clayton (315) 686-4123
Several exhibitions annually
Open Mon-Fri 9-5

TUPPER ARTS
106 Park Street, Tupper Lake (518) 359-5042 info@tupperarts.com

---

OTHER REFERENCES
Adirondack Regional Art Trail
www.northguide.org highlights off-the-beaten path studios and annual events, as well as museums and galleries with renowned exhibits.

BARN QUILT TRAILS
Barn Quilts are popping up all over rural America, and the North Country is no exception. Barn Quilts are painted on a single board and painted to look like quilt blocks. They are often hung on the exteriors of barns and other buildings, creating a trail for visitors to explore. For many, making barn quilts is a way to celebrate local heritage, identity, and community, to nurture local pride, and to encourage investment in beautifying and maintaining local properties. There are two extensive, well-established Barn Quilt Trails already in St. Lawrence County in Colton and Hammond, and people around the county and beyond are making more every day! **WWW.VISITSTLC.COM/BARNQUILTTRAILS** has a google map of barn quilt sites as well as maps for the Hammond and Colton trails.

Balloon Rides

ADIRONDACK BALLOON FLIGHTS (518) 793-6342 www.adkballoonflights.com
First hot air balloon company in New York State. Majestic balloon flights offer views of the Adirondacks, Lake George and the Saratoga areas. This is an unparalleled experience of flight.

CHAMPAGNE BALLOON ADVENTURES 27 James St., Alexandria Bay (315) 482-9356 www.balloonadventures.com Float a few feet from the water or soar 1,000 over the St. Lawrence. Hot air ballooning should not be missed!

Beaches

BLUE MOUNTAIN LAKE BEACH
3464 NY 28
Blue Mountain
(518) 648-5112

CADYVILLE BEACH
Route 3
Cadyville
(518) 562-6860

LAKE CLEAR BEACH
Route 30
Saranac Lake

LAKE COLBY BEACH
Lake Colby Drive
Saranac Lake

LAKE PLACID PUBLIC BEACH
801 Mirror Lake Drive
Lake Placid
(518) 523-2591

LONG LAKE PUBLIC BEACH
1258 Main St
Long Lake
(518) 624-3077

LISBON BEACH
9975 NY Route 37
Ogdensburg
(315) 393-5374

LITTLE WOLF BEACH
105 Wolf Pond Road
Tupper Lake
(518) 359-3000

MASSENA TOWN BEACH
1255 NY Route 131
Massena
(315) 764-0380

MIDDLE SARANAC LAKE BEACH
Route 30
Saranac Lake

NORWOOD BEACH
Lakeshore Drive
Norwood
(315) 353-9965

POSTWOOD PARK
Church St
Hannawa Falls
(315) 265-4030

SANDSTONER PARK
43 Pine Street
Potsdam
(315) 265-4030

TAYLOR PARK
Miner Street Road
Canton
(315) 386-3992

Bike Shops

**BLACK RIVER
ADVENTURERS SHOP**
129 Mill Street, Watertown
(315) 786-8800
www.blackriveradventures.com
repairs, rentals and sales

**CYCLES ENDURANCE
& SPORTS**
25 Market Street, Potsdam
(315) 274-0221
Mountain and Road Bike
Sales & Repairs
check their Facebook page
for seminars, group rides
and organized races

GRASSE RIVER OUTFITTERS
45 Main St., Canton
(315) 714-3255
Complete bike service,
all makes and models

HIGH PEAKS CYCLERY
2733 Main Street, Lake Placid
(518) 523-3764
www.highpeakscyclery.com

PLACID PLANET BICYCLES
2242 Saranac Avenue
Lake Placid
(518) 523-4128
www.placidplanet.com

Biking

FAMILY FRIENDLY BIKING

THE REMINGTON TRAIL, CANTON
3.2 mile paved loop that winds around the Partridge Run Golf Course. There is parking at the golf course parking lot off Sullivan Drive. (There is a playground just beyond the parking area).

SUNY POTSDAM When school is not in session, the Potsdam campus is a great place to take younger children to ride; lots of loops and ramps.

OGDENSBURG – MAPLE CITY TRAIL
Starting at the Ogdenburg Visitor's Center, 100 Riverside Drive, the 2.2 mile paved pathway follows the banks of the Oswegatchie River.

MASSENA Check out the Richards Landing Bike Trail and Whalen Park Trail that connect west of Massena at the Masssena Country Club. The almost three miles of paved pathway along the St. Lawrence River provide a scenic and family-friendly ride between the Massena Town Beach and Whalen Park – both attractive parks with beaches and facilities.

ROBERT MOSES STATE PARK Just northeast of Massena, offers a few quiet roads suitable for family biking. The park is located partly on the mainland and partly on Barnhart Island. The park is reached through a tunnel under the Eisenhower Lock.

SARANAC LAKE Roads, paths and trails at Fish Creek Campground.

BLOOMINGDALE BOG TRAIL A 10 mile flat ride following a former railroad bed along bogs and wetlands (mountain bike).

WATERTOWN Black River Trail is a paved scenic trail of 4.5 miles between Watertown and Black River, with parking available at either end. Directions at www.traillink.com

MORLEY-BUCKS BRIDGE- West Potsdam Loop – A 22 mile moderate loop, that takes you along the Grasse River through Morley to Bucks Bridge, then to West Potsdam and back to Canton through prime farmland.

OLD MILL TOWN LOOP – A 31 mile moderate loop through the towns of Canton and Potsdam, with visible mill ruins in the hamlet of Pyrites as a highlight.

LAMPSON FALLS LOOP – A 45 mile difficult loop through Canton, Clare, Pierrepont and Russell with a stop at scenic Lampson Falls.

PYRITES-OLD DEKALB ROAD – A 16 mile difficult loop taking the rider into a series of scenic hills south and west of Canton.

INDIAN CREEK TOUR – A 25 mile moderate loop taking the rider along flat to gently rolling country roads between Canton, Morley and Rensselaer Falls and completely around the Indian Creek Nature Center. Route 30, Malone to Tupper Lake, is 60 miles of wide (6 feet in most places) shoulders and light traffic. Stop for a picnic and swim at Meacham Lake.

RESOURCES

www.bikethebyways.org – biking the scenic byways of the Adirondack North Country

www.STLCtrails.com – detailed directions with trail maps for cycling routes and mountain biking trails.

www.Traillink.com – by Rails-to-Trails Conservancy

GROUPS

ADIRONDACK MOUNTAIN CLUB – LAURENTIAN CHAPTER – schedules outings (including biking) throughout the year. Membership is not required to participate and there is no charge. Their events calendar can be accessed at www.adklaurentian.org

CGSW RACING, OGDENSBURG – hold several events for cycling including Mini Maple Kids Triathlon, held annually in August. Find them on FaceBook

FRIENDS OF HIGLEY – "The Higley 100" - annual 100km century ride held in early September. Rides begin and end at Higley Trails Lodge in Higley Flow State Park, South Colton. There is also a 50k half century ride as well as shorter loops ranging from 2 to 25 miles which family and friends may enjoy while their century riders are on course.

Bird Watching

Northern New York's "crazy quilt" of habitats is home to a remarkable variety of birds, offering extraordinary opportunities for birding. Amateur and seasoned birders alike can enjoy looking for species living in mountains, forests, marshlands, grassy fields or meadows, still-water ponds and large open waters with bays.

Protected lands and undeveloped forests and meadows offer a safe nesting environment for many indigenous and migrating species.

NEAREST THE NORTH COUNTRY CHILDREN'S MUSEUM:

There are a variety of bird species you might sight as you wander the campus trails at Clarkson and St. Lawrence Universities. Tucked into the woods behind Clarkson (look for the water tower near the Adirondack lodge) are trails that can be done as a 1-2 mile loop. Easy walking, with the option to take a peek at the marshlands from a small lookout platform. The head of the Munter Trail (next to the Stewarts on Maple Street) is a short walk from the Children's Museum. It meanders for about 3 miles along the river and loops around near the Bayside Cemetery. It is a wide, level, packed sand trail and offers several elevated boardwalks that reach out on the river. There are also extensive trail networks on the St. Lawrence University campus. These start near Hulett and Jencks halls, weave through the nearby golf course, over elevated boardwalks, and through deep forest next to the Little River.

CLARKSON TRAILS MAP
www.clarksonathletics.com

ST. LAWRENCE UNIVERSITY TRAILS MAP
www.stlawu.edu

> You can use the New York Department of Environmental Conservation (DEC) Wildlife Management Area Bird Checklist as a way to keep track of your sightings! www.dec.ny.gov.

Driving north on routes 12 & 37 from Clayton to Massena, there are many state and municipal parks along the St. Lawrence River that are excellent birding spots. Read about some specified locations in the descriptions below. It is common to see Bald Eagles, Osprey, Common Mergansers, Common Goldeneye, Redheads, Ringed-Neck Ducks, Canvasbacks, Black Terns, American Bitterns, Cerulean Warblers, Common Terns, Bonaparte's Gulls, Great Blue Herons and many more waterfowl. The river is considered a significant wintering area for waterfowl where counts can easily reach in the thousands during the peak of fall and winter.

ZENDA FARMS
38973 Zenda Road, Clayton
www.tilandtrust.org Part of the 1000 Islands Land trust. A former dairy farm that operated through the 1950's, these pastures and hay meadows are conserved for a variety of nesting birds, including the Eastern Meadowlark, the Henslow's Sparrow, and Boblinks. Look out also for Great Horned, Screech, and Short-Eared Owls! The farm also serves as an education center and hosts a variety of family events including a community picnic and KidsTreks.

MINNA ANTHONY COMMON NATURE CENTER
44927 Cross Island Road, Fineview on Wellesley Island State Park
www.macnaturecenter.com Nine miles of trails to explore over 600 acres that encompass grassy meadows, wetlands, forests, and rocky outcrops. As well as bird-watching along the trails, the center has a butterfly house, nature exhibits, and other learning programs.

OTTER CREEK PRESERVE
193 Church Street,
Alexandria Bay www.tilandtrust.org
Part of the 1000 Islands Land trust.
About 2 miles of trails, some accessible, including a wildlife observation tower that overlooks the Golden-winged Warbler Demonstration Area.
Also look for Wood Ducks, Red-Winged Black Birds, and Great Blue Herons.

JACQUES CARTIER STATE PARK
Off Route 12, near Morristown
Part of the Upper St. Lawrence/1000 Islands Important Birding Area (IBA). Look for wintering waterfowl and migratory birds.

RED BARN PRESERVE
518 River Road East, Morristown
A Blue Heron rookery with over 60 active nests! It's about a quarter mile hike from the entrance to the boardwalk viewing area.

While here, explore the nearby Gateway Museum
www.morristowngatewaymuseum.org
which offers educational displays and some events.
Closes for the season in September.

SPARROWHAWK POINT
Off Route 37, Waddington
More than 3,000 nesting pairs of Bank Swallows make their home here (one of the largest colonies in the world!).

COLES CREEK STATE PARK
Route 37, Waddington
Look for Bald Eagles, Osprey, and migratory birds. A good spot to access the river and head south toward Sparrowhawk Point.

WILSON HILL WILDLIFE MANAGEMENT AREA
From Route 131
off Route 37 just south of Massena in Louisville
Trails and water access.
1.5 miles of the Nichols trail are handicap accessible and there are three accessible spur trails off the main trail that lead to viewing locations off the shoreline. There are two observation towers. Over 3,000 acres of open water pools bordered by cattail, shrub swamp, forest and meadows. Look for nesting and migrating waterfowl.

ROBERT MOSES STATE PARK / NICANDRI NATURE CENTER
19 Robinson Bay Road,
Massena
www.massenanaturecenter.com
Free admission to exhibits and programs. Handicap accessible trails. Look for waterfowl, upwards of 20 species of migratory birds; wading, shore, and song birds; Bald Eagles and Osprey.

Also be sure to explore these nearby areas:

GRAND LAKE RESERVE
45701 Burns Road, Redwood
www.indianriverlakes.org
A significant 1000-plus acres of publically accessible conserved land.

A variety of trails to explore and a canoe launch. Look for Eagles, Loons, Osprey, Blue Herons, Woodpeckers, Golden-Winged Warbler, Whip-poor-will, and a multitude of other bird species.

FISH CREEK MARSH WILDLIFE MANAGEMENT AREA/BLACK LAKE
Off Route 184 or Route 58,
Macomb
No developed hiking trails.
A boat-access location (two canoe launches and a larger boat launch). Over 2,000 acres of natural wetland and forested upland, as well as 93 acres of open grassland that is maintained for ground nesting birds.

Look for Golden-winged and Cerulean Warblers, Sedge Wren, Pied-billed Grebe, American Bittern, Least Bittern, Osprey, Bald Eagle, Loon, Turkey, Grouse, Northern Harrier and Whip-poor-will.

UPPER AND LOWER LAKES WILDLIFE MANAGEMENT AREA / INDIAN CREEK NATURE CENTER
Off County Route 14, Canton
www.indiancreeknaturecenter.us
Part of the Lisbon Grasslands Important Birding Area (IBA). Nature trails here are handicapped accessible. Mostly private land accessed through managed areas. Look for Pied-billed Grebe, American Bittern, Least Bittern, Northern Harrier, Black Tern, Sedge Wren, LeConte's and Nelson's Sharp-tailed Sparrows.

PAUL SMITH'S COLLEGE VISITOR INTERPRETIVE CENTER (VIC)
8023 State Route 30, Paul Smiths
www.paulsmiths.edu
A wide variety of birds make this their seasonal or year-round home (too many to list!) There are miles of trails that wander through forests and wetlands.

The Barnum Brook trail is fully accessible, and winds through the forest nearby a babbling brook, over boardwalks and even up to a marshland viewing platform.

There are many kid-friendly wildlife and nature exhibits, activities, and events and the center hosts the annual Great Adirondack Birding Celebration each May-June. This is a three-day event offering birding workshops, and guided field walks and paddles. There is also a butterfly house to visit in the summer months.

**Explore Cornell University's Ornithology Lab ebird to learn more about the birds you see and help identify them through descriptions, photos, videos, and audio clips.
www.ebird.org**

Boat Rentals

There are all types of water for canoes, kayaks, and larger motorboats. The Cranberry Lake region, one of the largest remote areas in the state, is for great paddlers. Spend the day on the St. Lawrence River boating and enjoy the boating, swimming or fishing. Along the way you can visit the many communities that have much to offer such as Sackets Harbor, Clayton and many more. You can also enjoy the many lakes, rivers and ponds that have beautiful scenery with many campsites and cabins if you decide to stay.

ADIRONDACK LAKES AND TRAILS OUTFITTERS
541 Lake Flower Avenue in Saranac Lake
(518) 891-7450
www.adirondackoutfitters.com
Offers canoe, kayak, and SUP rentals, as well as Adirondack guiding and instruction.

APS BOAT RENTALS
35593 County Rd 46, Theresa
(315) 486-2795
Boat rental service in Jefferson County.

AQUA MANIA INC
45765 NY-12, Alexandria Bay
(315) 482-4678
www.aqua-mania.com
Many different types of boats are available for rental. A security deposit is required on a credit card. All safety and coast guard equipment will be provided for your safety. Reservations are suggested.

BAYSIDE MARINA
1044 State St, Clayton
(315) 686-2121
www. bayside-marina.com
 Offering a variety of power boats including bow riders and cabin cruisers to rent and explore the 1000 Islands.

CLAYTON MARINA SALES & SERVICE
50 State Street, Clayton
(315) 686-3378
www.claytonmarina.com
Offering a large variety of rental boats to enjoy a day fishing, swimming, or sightseeing.

HARBOR'S END MARINA
8043 County Route 178, Henderson
(315) 938-5425
www.harborsendmarina.com
Offering large variety of rental boats. Reservations can be made with a deposit that will be applied to total rental amount. Must be 21 years of age or older. Refundable security deposit is required at time of rental. Fuel used or any damage incurred while renting is not included in rental rate.

HIGLEY OUTFITTERS
3906 State Highway 56, South Colton
(315) 216-7760
www.higley-outfitters.business.site
River outfitter offering canoe, kayak and stand up paddle board rentals specializing in high quality boats and boards for the most enjoyable paddling experiences possible. Worry free delivery and pickup along with pointers on where to go for all ages and skill levels.

KD KAYAK RENTALS
24912 Mullin Road, Dexter
(315) 771-2317
www.kdkayakrentals.com
They offer kayak and paddleboard rentals. Lifejackets are included in the rental.

LAKESIDE GENERAL STORE AND BOAT RENTALS
7140 NY-3, Cranberry Lake
(315) 848-2501
www.campersvillage.tripod.com
 Offering rented pontoon boats, small fishing boats and more. The store carries grocery essentials, gas, souvenirs and camping supplies. Within 4 miles are Big Bog Island, Hawks Island, Hedgehog Bay and Pond and Shanty Rock Flow for a variety of boating locations. If you want

to stay at Starkey's Point camp, bring your own boat, rent a boat or arrange for a water taxi at Cranberry Lake Dry Dock & Marine Service. The camp is boat access only. Boaters must wear personal flotation devices.

MARTIN'S MARINA
28491 County Route 6, Cape Vincent
(315) 654-3104 www.martinsmarina.com
Full-Service Marina, authorized dealer for Lund Boats, Avalon Pontoons, Mercury Outboards, Mercruiser Stem Drives, Shoreland's Trailer, Docks and Hoist, Mud Bay.

MUSKIE MAGIC FISHING CHARTERS
18 Richards St., Massena
(315) 769-7683, www.muskiemagic.com.
Charter a boat for fishing or enjoy the scenery. Handicapped accessible.

RAQUETTE RIVER OUTFITTERS
1754 State Route 30, Tupper Lake
(518) 359-3228
www.raquetteriveroutfitters.com
They rent and sell canoes, kayaks, SUPs, camping gear, lightweight pack canoes, paddles, maps and accessories.

**RIVERBAY BOAT
AND KAYAK RENTALS**
97 New Road, Chippewa Bay
(315) 579-8174 www.riverbayrentals.com
Renting boats, kayaks and standup paddle boards.

RIVERVIEW OF WADDINGTON
12508 Route 37, Waddington
(315) 388-5912
www.riverviewofwaddingtonmotel.com
Kayak and boat rentals.

**STONEBRIDGE KAYAK
AND CANOE RENTAL**
1833 State Highway 345, Madrid
(315) 322-4856

ST. REGIS CANOE OUTFITTERS
73 Dorsey Street, Saranac Lake
(518) 891-1838
www.canoeoutfitters.com
Lightweight canoe and kayak rentals, shuttles and quality camping gear rentals, maps and guidebooks, guided trips.

**THREE RIVERS KAYAK
AND CANOE RENTALS**
558 Pontoon Bridge Road, Massena
(315) 250-7374
www.threeriversparks.org
Watercraft rentals of all types for all mobility levels.

THE WANDERING KAYAK
Theresa
(315) 628-5751
www.thewanderingkayak.com
Based in Theresa, they are a wandering mobile kayak service. Check their website or call to find out where they'll be each day. They will also bring kayaks to your chosen location.

WELLESLEY ISLAND BOAT RENTALS
46338 County Road 100, Wellesley Island
(315) 507-0755
www.wiboatrentals.com
Rental experts will assist you in selecting the right boat. Variety of boats and kayaks available.

**NY BOATING
LAWS AND REGULATIONS**
www.boat-ed.com
Visit the above site to learn everything you need to know for any laws and restrictions, including age and operation restrictions, the NYS Parks Adventure Program, and where to take the boaters course.

BOAT LAUNCH SITES
www.dec.ny.gov
You can also visit the Department of Environmental Conservation website for a complete list of boat launch sites.

Boat Tours

In the 1000 Islands, one of the most popular attractions in the region, a scenic cruise will let you explore the many islands and marvel at the beautiful scenery. The region's many boat lines offer a variety of cruises, ranging from one hour to five hours. You can travel on a modern glass-topped catamaran or triple-decker cruise boats, paddle-wheel riverboats or an historic 1929 vintage wooden cruise boat. Delight in touring past and visiting some of the fairytale castles, stately mansions and historic lighthouses. Your tour guide will entertain you with many true stories of pirates and bootleggers and give you a history of the beautiful waterfront properties dotting the landscape.

The cruising season runs from May through the fall color season of October. Most lines offer frequent scheduled departures and are narrated, providing commentary on the history and lore of the 1000 Islands. Typical cruise boats offer food and beverage service aboard, and have enclosed, climate-controlled decks, as well as open-air decks. Specialty cruises including sunset, dinner and luncheon cruises are also available. Private charters are also available.

TIPS: SOME CRUISES REQUIRE A PASSPORT OR VISA. BE SURE TO CHECK IN ADVANCE THAT YOURS IS VALID.

Cruises leaving from Alexandria Bay, Clayton, Gananoque, Ivy Lea and Rockport touring the central part of the 1000 Islands region of the St. Lawrence. Many of these cruises offer a stop-over at historic Boldt Castle on Heart Island, or Singer Castle on Dark Island. Tours leaving from Kingston cruise the western area of the 1000 Islands region between Kingston and Gananoque. Tours leaving from Brockville cruise the eastern area of the 1000 Islands. Check to see if your cruise requires a Passport or Visa.

1000 ISLANDS & SEAWAY CRUISES
Blockhouse Island, Brockville, Ontario
(613) 345-7333, 800-353-3157
www.1000islandscruises.rezgo.com

Select from one of the three tours offered to enjoy a 1000 Island tour. Passports or valid Visa required for US citizens. Croisiere 'Castle Prowler Adrenisland' Cruise (2 hours) offers a unique cruising experience. When at faster speeds, enjoy classic rock soundtrack, and the Captain's commentary during slower portions of the tour. It is a fun-filled experience that covers 42 miles and features views of Boldt Castle, Singer Castle, three historic lighthouses, the Shortest International Bridge and more! Licensed beverage and snack bar service available.

Croisiere 'Jewels of the St. Lawrence' Cruise (1.5 hours) offers an informative introductory cruise with frequent departures featuring the Eastern Group of the 1000 Island, the St Lawrence Seaway Millionaire's Row and Brockville's historic waterfront. 'St. Lawrence Soiree' Dinner Cruise (2 hours) Take a memorable cruise while listening to the highlights of the Captain's commentary. You can take in the magnificent views of castles, islands and much more. Have a relaxed and casual buffet dinner and see the beautiful sunset and Brockville's skyline by night. Featuring dinner music.

1000 ISLANDS WATER TAXI
47329 Westminister Park Road, Wellesey Island, Alexandria Bay
(315) 727-1939
www.1000islandsscenictours.com

This private service provides a leisurely scenic cruise on the beautiful St. Lawrence River and attractions like Boldt Castle. The company's 26-foot authentic wooden Lyman boat "Apache," a smaller vessel can navigate to sights that larger tours cannot access. They will customize the cruise to your preferences and can carry up to six passengers of your own party. Bring your own refreshments.

CLAYTON ISLAND TOURS,
39621 Chateau Lane, Clayton

(315) 686-4820
www.claytonislandtours.com
Clayton Island Tours offer three different tours of the 1000 Islands. *The Rock Island Glass Bottom Boat Tour* takes you to Rock Island Lighthouse, one of six lights put up along the St Lawrence River to guide traffic to and from Lake Ontario through the waterway. *A Boldt Castle* and *Two-Nations Tour* is a unique 25-mile tour that includes a stop at Boldt Castle. Two-Nation Lunch Cruise that stops at Boldt Castle and Rock Island. Tour Boldt Castle to learn the romantic history of Heart Island, visit Rock Island Lighthouse and walk the grounds. Enjoy the food of the different cruises that include a Wine and Cheese Twilight Cruise and pizza and wing cruises for families and adults. Learn about the origins of Thousand Islands salad dressing, which was developed by a local fisherman's wife gained national attention after George Boldt served it in the Waldorf Astoria Hotel in New York City; Grindstone Island, where River Rat cheese got its name; and the 1000 Island International Bridge that connects New York to Canada.

GANANOQUE - GANANOQUE BOAT LINE, 100 Water Street, Ontario
(613) 382-2114, (888) 717-4837
www.ganboatline.com
Enjoy a tour of the 1000 Islands aboard one of the five triple-decker vessels with indoor and outdoor seating. Food and beverage, snacks, restrooms and indoor/outdoor seating are available. First level handicapped accessible. Passports and valid Visas are required for all US citizens. Gananoque Boat Lines has four different cruises to choose from. *The Original Heart of the 1000 Islands Cruise* is a 1-hour cruise that takes you by fifth and sixth generation family island cottages and navigate through the beautiful narrow channels. *The Lost Ships of the 1000 Islands Cruise* is a 2.5-hour tour that combines video and audio commentary with side-scan sonar images of seven sunken ships. Cruise by Boldt Castle on Heart Island and sail by the homes of the rich and famous on "Millionaire's Row." *The Boldt Castle Stopover* is a 5-hour cruise that takes you through the American span of the 1000 Islands. You will have a 2-hour stopover at Boldt Castle on Heart Island to tour the Castle and learn the romantic history of Boldt Castle. See the sights of the St. Lawrence River and cruise by the homes of the rich and famous on "Millionaire's Row." Your return voyage will take you through the Canadian Span of the 1000 Islands. Located at 280 Main Street, Gananoque, Ontario (minutes across the 1000 Island International bridge) *The Landmarks of the 1000 Islands Cruise* (located at 95 Ivy Lea Road, Lansdowne, Ontario) is a 1-hour cruise that will show you the 1000 Island International Bridge, Zavikon Islands and the Statue of St. Lawrence, that is only visible from the water. Located at 95 Ivy Lea Road, Lansdowne, Ontario (minutes across the 1000 Island International Bridge)

GARNSEY'S CLASSIC ISLAND CRUISES
French Bay Marina, 530 Theresa Street, Clayton (315) 955-9166
www.classicislandcruises.com
Charter a half- or full-day fishing trip aboard the Muskie, a fully equipped fishing boat. They also feature their Wine and Cheese Cruises that accommodate up to six passengers and runs for 3.5 to 4 hours and includes a bottle of Coyote Moon wine and a platter of local meats and cheeses. This cruise will stop at several shopping locations along the way.

HOME'S FERRY, 319 Club Street, Cape Vincent (315) 783-0638, (613) 385-2402
www.hferry.com, www.wolfeisland.com
This is a family-operated business that transports vehicles or passengers on foot to Wolfe Island, Ontario. It is the only international auto/passenger ferry on the St. Lawrence River. Wolfe Island is the largest

Island of the 1000 islands. Take a scenic ride across the St Lawrence River, then either take a short drive or short ferry ride to spend the day at Wolfe Island. Enjoy the corn maze, golfing, fishing, hiking, or attend one of the many annual events. If you are there in the evening, you will see a breath-taking sunset. A fun-filled experience for your family. Don't forget to bring your camera! Passports or Visa Required.

LAKE EFFECT CHARTERS
320 Dodge Avenue, Sackets Harbor
(315) 804-3864, (315) 646-6033
www.visit1000islands.com
They offer sightseeing cruises, sunset cruises, light house cruises and swimming around Henderson Harbor, Henderson Bay, Black River Bay, Sackets Harbor and Chaumont Bay.

LAKE SAINT LAWRENCE BOAT TOURS
20 Main Street, Waddington
(315) 388-5253
www.visitadirondacks.com
Sit back and enjoy an ecological and historical narrated tour of Lake St. Lawrence, a unique section of the St Lawrence River. You can select from the dinner cruise, fishing excursion or private charter. Cruise on Nature's Way Coast Guard Certified, 38-foot commercial pontoon boat. Rest rooms, snacks and beverages are available on board. Handicapped accessible. Reservations recommended for fishing and historical tours. Reservations required for the dinner cruises.

ROCKPORT BOAT LINE CRUISES
20 Front Street, Rockport, Ontario, Canada (613) 659-3402, 800-563-8687
www.rockportcruises.com
Enjoy one of the many cruises offered of the 1000 Islands. They offer three different types of cruises, the Sightseeing Cruise, Dining Cruise, Castle Cruise. Passports required for all their cruises! The Sightseeing Cruise will showcase the major features of the islands including: Zavikon Island, Boldt Castle, Millionaire's Row, Canadian Palisades and the 1000 Islands International Bridge. The Sightseeing cruises range from one, two or 2.5 hours. The Dining Cruises offer you two different experiences to enjoy the St. Lawrence River and 1000 Islands. The two-hour day cruise offers you a delicious country buffet for lunch and the 2.5- hour sunset cruise offers a delicious dinner at sunset in the Main Salon. You can enjoy the panoramic views from both levels of the Double Decker Cruise Ship. The 2.5 Hour Sunset Dinner Cruise is only offered on Saturday evenings. Reservations and pre-payment are required.

SCHERMERHORN HARBOR SHUTTLE
71 Schermerhorn Landing, Hammond
(315) 324-5966
www.schermerhornharbor.com
The Schermerhorn Harbor Shuttle offers a 45-minute guided tour of Singer Castle on Dark Island. All guided tours leave the main gate on the hour. Young children must be carried by adults. Children under 4 are free.

Two-Castle Cruise
If you like castles, try the all-day enchanting Two Castle Tour of both Boldt Castle located on Heart Island and Singer Castle on Dark Island. A picnic basket lunch is served onboard. Reservations and pre-payment are required for this cruise.

Three boat tours –The Fulton Chain of Lakes, Raquette Lake and Big Moose Lake all offer their own history of the area. Tour boats on the Fulton Chain of Lakes and Raquette Lake also offer dinner cruises and have other special features:

BIG MOOSE LAKE TOURS
1500 Big Moose Road, Eagle Bay
(315) 357-3532
www.dunnsboats.com
Experience the beauty and history of Big Moose Lake. A personal guide will take you back in time to learn about the famous murder in the Adirondacks that inspired Theodore Dreiser's novel, *An American Tragedy*, and the movie "A Place in The Sun." You will also learn about Big Moose Lake and its unique camps, scenery and history. They offer a dinner cruise in the evenings to the Big Moose Inn after you have enjoyed your cruise on the Lake.

OLD FORGE: OLD FORGE LAKE CRUISES, Route 28, Old Forge, (315) 369-6473
www.oldforgelakecruises.com
Cruise on the first four lakes of the Fulton Chain of Lakes. You will board the Uncas or the Clearwater for a 28-mile scenic cruise. The narration features the history and folklore of the Central Adirondacks. Enjoy the many different cruises offered: Mailboat Cruise, Children's Cruise, Dinner Cruise, Evening "Showboat" Cruises.

RAQUETTE LAKE NAVIGATION TOURS
224 Main Street, Raquette Lake
www.raquettelakenavigation.com
Take a ride on one of the many cruises offered on Raquette Lake. Try the 90-minute Sightseeing Cruise of Raquette Lake and enjoy the beautiful scenery of the Adirondacks while getting some great photo shots. You can select from their Special Events cruise which changes for each event or one of their Dining Cruises for some of the most delicious meals, beautiful scenery and magnificent sunsets.

UNCLE SAM BOAT TOURS
45 James St., Alexandria Bay
(315) 482-2611, 800-253-9229,
1-888-ALEXBAY
www.usboattours.com
Uncle Sam Boat Tours offer a variety of excursions to experience. Select from their Luncheon Tour, Dinner Tour, Sip n' Sail Tour, Two Nations Tour and the Craft Beer and Wine Tours. Completely open top decks. Heated, glass enclosed lower decks for Spring and Fall cruising comfort. No passports or visas required. Professional Tour Guides. Lunch and Dinner Cruises. Unlimited stopovers at Boldt Castle. U.S. Coast Guide inspected and approved. Handicapped accessible.

The Two Nations Tour takes visitors on a 22-mile trip through American and Canadian waters. You will stop at Heart Island for self-guided tours of Boldt Caste. Single, double and triple-deck vessels can hold up to 425 people traveling Millionaire's Row on both sides of the border, visiting Boldt Castle and islands where other palatial homes once stood.

This is the only tour from Alexandria Bay that travels through the Canadian section of the Islands. The castles have separate admission fees.

The Craft Beer and Wine Tour where you will sample some great craft beers and local wine as you marvel at the beautiful sunset and enjoy the dancing with live entertainment.

Sip n' Sail Tour takes you on a magical evening cruise along the Thousand Islands. A great date night cruise to enjoy the river in the early evening, then have a romantic dinner at the one of the many restaurants within walking distance of the boat line docks.

Luncheon Cruise lets you relax on a leisurely cruise through the channels of the Thousand islands to learn about the region's rich history and enjoy a delicious buffet. If you are interested, you can tour Boldt Castle at the end of the cruise.

Dinner Cruise offers an unforgettable evening cruising some of the most romantic channels in the Thousand Islands. Enjoy seeing the ships of many nations and the beautiful island homes   You will be wined, dined, and entertained for two and a half hours.

YOUR WAVE TOURS
1045 State Street, Clayton
(315) 778-8128
www.yourwavetours.com
Rent a private pontoon boat on the St Lawrence River and enjoy the ride. They will customize your tour from a dance party, beach party, karaoke trip or a relaxing scenic tour.

Bookstores

THE BIRCHBARK BOOKSHOP
40 Ashton Road, Potsdam
(315) 265-3875
www.birchbarkbookshop.com
A used bookstore with over 75,000 books from every genre as well as a selection of first editions and rare books. Wander through the maze of rustic bookshelves or cozy up with a book in a comfy chair by the woodstove. Limited weekend hours only. Cash only.

THE BOOKSTORE PLUS
2491 Main Street, Lake Placid
(518) 523-2950
www.thebookstoreplus.com
An independent bookstore specializing in the best new releases,and largest selection of Adirondack literature anywhere. Art supplies,notebooks, and greeting cards also available.

Art supplies and notebooks as well as greeting cards also available.

THE BOOK NOOK
7A Broadway, Saranac Lake
(518) 354-8439
This small space offers a surprising wealth of new books in many genres from fiction to manga. They hold a monthly book club for grownups, as well as storytime and craft events for kids. Their Facebook page gives all the details. **Bonus treat: have fun exploring Goody Goody's, a great toy and game store, two doors down.**

BREWER BOOKSTORE
(St. Lawrence University)
92 Park Street, Canton
(315) 229-5460
www.brewerbookstore.com
A large variety of new books for all ages, as well as gifts, stationery, art and computer supplies. They also have a small café offering gourmet coffee, tea and baked treats and periodically host a variety of musical events and lectures.

THE COMPUTER GUYS
7585 US Highway 11 Potsdam
(315) 265-3866
Along with selling and repairing all types of computers, this store buys and sells textbooks.

FRIENDS OF THE POTSDAM PUBLIC LIBRARY BOOKSTORE
2 Park Street, Potsdam
(basement of Potsdam Civic Center)
Though officially open only on Saturdays 10am-1pm, a volunteer oftenstaffs the store during the week also (if the sign is out, they're open!).There is always a large rotating collection of used books to choose from, and lots of kid's books and puzzles.

Always a large rotating collection of used books to choose from, and lots of kid's books and puzzles.

PAPERBACK BROWSER
11484 US Highway 11
North Lawrence
(315) 389-4900
Half-price used paperback books.

TREE OF LIFE CHRISTIAN BOOKSTORE
809 County Route 34, Potsdam
(315) 261-4203
www.treeoflifebooksandgifts.com
New and used books, Bibles, study guides, music and videos, gifts, local crafts, and supplies for children, youth, and adult classes. It is located in an old one-room schoolhouse built in the 1800's!

THE UNIVERSITY BOOKSTORE
(Clarkson University)
39 Market Street, Potsdam
(315) 265-9260
www.bkstr.com
Amongst all the Clarkson 'spirit' wear, you'll find a small but worthy offering of books for all ages, as well as stationery and office supply basics.

Bowling Alleys

Always call ahead for open bowling times:

1. **BIG D'S HOUSE**, 2348 County Route 5, Moira, (518) 529-6001

2. **CHATEAUGAY COMMUNITY BOWLING CENTER**, 191 E. Main St., Chateaugay, (518) 497-6581

3. **HARRISVILLE LANES**, Church & Main St., Harrisville, (315) 543-2775

4. **HEUVELTON BOWLING CENTER**, Heuvelton-Flackville Rd., Heuvelton, (315) 344-7070 open bowling Fridays 6-10 pm

5. **LAKEVIEW LANES & THE FOUL LINE SPORTSBAR**, 1939 New York 30, Tupper Lake, (518) 359-2234

6. **LUCKY STRIKE LANES**, 36 Woodward St., Malone, (518) 483-5220
www.luckystrikemalone.com

7. **MARKET LANES**, 144 Market St., Potsdam, (315) 265-9210

8. **OGDENSBURG BOWLING**, 1121 Patterson St., Ogdensburg, (315) 388-4462

9. **PINE PLAINS BOWLING ALLEY**, 4320 Conway Rd., Fort Drum, (315) 772-6601
www.drum.armymwr.com

10. **PLA-MOR LANES**, 577 State St., Watertown, (315) 786-3356
www.plamorlanesny.com

11. **THERESA BOWLING CENTER**, 38530 NY-37, Theresa, (315) 628-5614

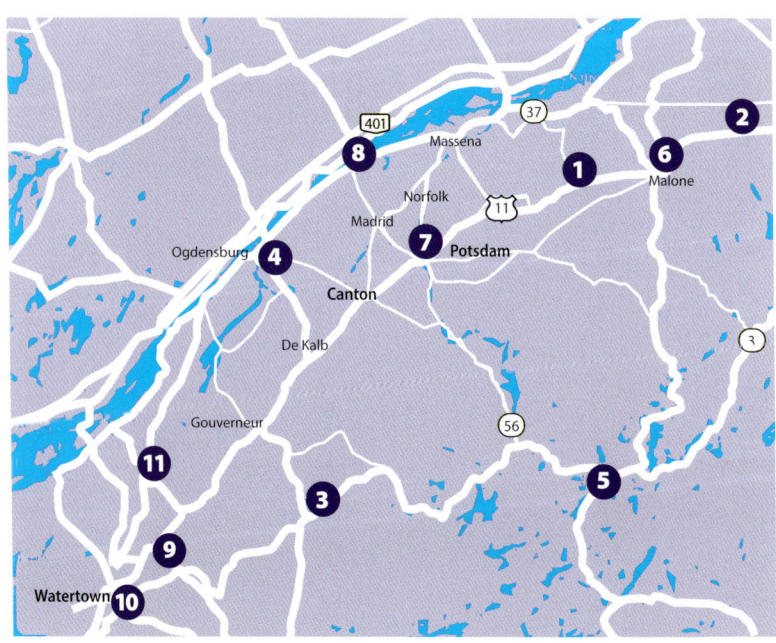

26 Canoeing, Kayaking, and Rowing

Few areas offer so many rivers with such easy and numerous access points. As the rivers rush out of the mountains they never fully settle down. Waterfalls and low water rapids are numerous along all rivers, and dams often block the way, although portages around them are usually short. You hardly need a guide to canoe or kayak in the area. Every stretch is worth exploring and usually has easy access. Here are a few to get you started:

NEW YORK STATE LAW REQUIRES THAT ALL PADDLERS WEAR A COAST GUARD APPROVED LIFE JACKET (a PFD - a Personal Flotation Device) anytime between November 1 and May 1, and all paddlers under the age of 12 must always wear a life jacket of appropriate size. See NYS Nav. Law Section 40.1

THE GRASSE RIVER AND LITTLE RIVER

The Grasse River and Little River provide excellent canoeing opportunities. Throughout the year the St. Lawrence Valley Paddlers Club offers a variety of canoeing and kayaking events. In the spring, Canton is home to the Rushton Canoe Races that attract hundreds of visitors, as well as the Canton Canoe Weekend. For more information on canoeing, including a calendar of events and a swap shop, visit the club's website at **www.slvpaddlers.org**.

THE RACQUETTE RIVER

The Racquette River (sometimes spelled Raquette) is approximately 170 miles long and is the second-longest river in New York state. The area is rich in history, dating back to escapes to Canada during the Revolutionary War and frequent travel in the mid-1800s.

Brookfield Power maintains recreation areas within the Racquette River Recreation Corridor, which includes 19 public access sites with boat access, fishing, picnic areas, camping and whitewater boating. The trek can be as brief as several hours or as long as several days. Brookfield Power encourages paddlers to be safe, avoiding areas such as dams, intake structures, gates, water conveyance structures, powerhouses and substations.

Access sites on the Racquette River Recreation Corridor are at Piercefield, Carry Falls Dam Site, Stark Hydroelectric Facility, Blake Boat, McNeil Campsite, Blake Hydroelectric Facility, Rainbow Falls Hydroelectric Facility, Five Falls Hydroelectric Facility, South Colton Reservoir Recreation Site, Higley Flow Picnic Area and Boat Launch, Stone Valley Trail, Sugar Island Day-use Area in Potsdam, Norwood Boat Launch, Yaleville Hydroelectric Facility near the village of Norwood, East Norfolk Canoe Portage and the Raymondville Cartop Boat Launch. A map of access sites, including details of services available at each site, is available at the St. Lawrence County Chamber of Commerce, 101 Main Street Canton.
(877) 228-7810, **www.visitslc.com**

THE OSWEGATCHIE RIVER

The Oswegatchie River is one of the largest and longest rivers in the North Country region. The river allows paddlers to access the river at several key locations including Balsam Pond to the Grasse River, Tooley Pond, Chaumont Pond and the Oswegatchie River in Newton Falls, Flat Rock, Town of Fine, Sucker Lake, Oswegatchie Little River off Youngs Road in Star Lake, Inlet in Star Lake, Nicks Pond, Star Lake and Streeter Lake, Star Lake.

More paddling information in St. Lawrence County, including brochures and maps, is available at the St. Lawrence County Chamber of Commerce at 101 Main Street in Canton, New York **(877) 228-7810**
www.visitstlc.com

THE ADIRONDACK PARK

The Adirondack Park has 6,800 miles of rivers, 1,200 miles of which have been designated by the state as Wild, Scenic and Recreational Rivers. Some areas in the Adirondack Forest Preserve are limited to non-motorized watercraft and may be miles in from paved roads.

THE ST. REGIS CANOE AREA

Near Saranac Lake, the St. Regis canoe area, with 57 interconnecting lakes and ponds, offers a unique wilderness experience. The popular Adirondack Canoe Route starts at Old Forge and follows a string of lakes, ponds and rivers, and portages nearly 140 miles to Tupper and the Saranac Lakes.

For more information on camping permits and guides to Adirondack Canoe Routes see the website www.dec.ny.gov

The NYS Department of Environmental Conservation Bureau of Forest Resource Management 625 Broadway 5th Floor Albany, N.Y. 12233 (518) 402-9428

Calendars of Events

Northern New York enjoys a rich cultural life.
These community calendars can help you find just what you need on any given day.

www.adirondack.net
www.adklaurentian.org – group led cycling and hiking excursions
www.natureupnorth.org – event calendar for group outdoor activities
www.ncpr.org North Country Public Radio – (from homepage: more/calendar)
www.northcountrynow.com (web companion to *North Country This Week*) – 7 day calendar.
North Country This Week – free weekly paper, published on Tuesdays. Home deliveries and stocked at many business locations

www.visitmalone.com
www.visitstlc.com
www.wwnytv.com

Cider Mills

BURRVILLE CIDER MILL, INC.,
18176 County Route 156, Watertown
(315) 788-7292; (866) 612-1980
www.burrvillecidermill.com

Burrville Cider Mill built in 1801, is one of Jefferson County's oldest establishments. For a fun-filled day, tour the mill and be greeted by the sweet smell of North Country apple cider and fresh cider donuts, still too hot to touch. All visitors are encouraged to take a stroll on the decks overlooking the falls. You will feel the mist on your face and can hear the roar of the falls. It is an experience you will not forget. You can watch them press the best Sweet Apple Cider the North Country has to offer. Cider is pressed every Tuesday, Thursday, Saturday and Sunday, best times are between 10 a.m. and noon. Take a self-guided tour while you are there.

Cross-Country (Nordic) Ski Trails

> **TIPS:**
> One of the best places for cross-country skiing in the area is Higley Flow State Park in South Colton, where skiers of all ages and abilities can enjoy the camp roads and trails through the woods and along the Racquette River. The roads and trails are groomed and track-set after each snowfall. The Friends of Higley organization of volunteers offers a daily e-mail update on trail conditions and other winter events. To receive updates, email info@higleyfriends.org. A youth ski club called the Ermines is offered through the Friends of Higley. More information and a map of the roads and trails can be found at **www.higleyfriends.org**

Northern New York is a great place to enjoy winter, with many groomed trails for cross-country skiing and snowshoeing. For a map of some of the best trails in St. Lawrence County, visit the St. Lawrence County Chamber of Commerce website at **www.stlctrails.com**.

Here is a sampling of the best trails in the northern New York area:

BRASHER STATE FOREST off County Road 50, Brasher Falls, or Route 11 at St. Lawrence Central School. **www.dec.ny.gov**

SUNY CANTON 15 kilometers of trails, accessed from Parking Lot 6 across from French Hall, bear left at the Y.

CATAMOUNT FOREST 9 miles south of South Colton on the east side of State Route 56. Limited parking available at Catamount Mountain trailhead, just south of the lodge driveway. Groomed trails open to the public, **www.catamountlodge.com**

CLARKSON UNIVERSITY 5 miles of trails, accessible from the parking lot on hill campus by Center for Advanced Materials Processing (CAMP) by the big green water tower. Bathrooms are available on the first floor of the Outdoor Lodge. **www.clarkson.edu**.

Cranberry Lake Area:
THE FIVE PONDS WILDERNESS AREA, southwest of Cranberry Lake is one of the most remote and least-used areas of New York State. Details and maps are available at the New York State DEC website at **www.dec.ny.gov**

Penetration of this area in winter is a true test of wilderness skills. It is suitable only for people who carry and know how to

use field repair materials and survival equipment. There are about 40 miles of trails in this area. Starting point is the Village of Wanakena, which is 2 miles south of NY Route 3. The turnoff to Wanakena is 4 miles east of Benson Mines, and 8 miles west of Cranberry Lake. In Wanakena, cross a one-lane bridge across the Oswegatchie River. The High Falls truck trail goes straight ahead.

FOR THE DEAD CREEK FLOW TRUCK TRAIL, turn left after crossing the bridge, and go one-half mile beyond. The Dead Creek Flow route covers more interesting terrain and reaches Dead Creek Flow, a long narrow arm of Cranberry Lake in about 2 miles. A red marked hiking trail goes around the end of the Flow to a lean-to on the opposite shore. The High Falls truck trail is generally level for most of its length.

THE LEARY TRAIL, blue markers, branches to the left in 1.4 miles. In combination with the truck trail, it is possible to make a loop trail of nine miles. As the Leary trail contains a number of ups and downs, this route is rated expert.

CRANBERRY LAKE WILD FOREST PEAVINE SWAMP SKI TRAIL, begins on the south side of Route 3 east of Peavine Swamp. The main trail (3.9 miles) leads to the state lean-to on Inlet Flow. There are two loops at either end (3.4 miles and 12 miles) and a 2.1 mile loop in the middle. Fort Jackson State Forest, Town of Stockholm. www.dec.ny.gov

GLENMEAL STATE FOREST TOWN OF PIERREPONT, off County Road 24, accessed from Route 68. Access also from Dillabough Road. The total distance of the trail system is 1.9 miles and is geared toward the novice to moderate skier. Once on the trail it is possible to venture into a variety of loops which all interconnect. www.dec.ny.gov

HIGLEY FLOW STATE PARK, Off Route 56, two miles east of South Colton. A variety of trails are offered including 9.3 miles (15k) trackset for classical, 4.3 miles (7k) groomed for freestyle and 1.9 miles (3k) backcountry trails. There is no charge for skiing in the park, however there is a trail register located adjacent to the parking lot which skiers are asked to sign in to keep a record of trail usage. Trail Information and map available. (315) 262-2880. www.parks.ny.gov

HIGH FLATS STATE FOREST PARISHVILLE, from County Road 58, right on Rodwell Mill Road, left jog to Crowley Road, 4.5 miles of trails, 2.6 miles of unplowed road used to complete the loop. www.parks.ny.gov

LENNY ROAD PARISHVILLE, 7 km. of trails.

PEAVINE SWAMP SKI TRAIL, State Highway 3, west of Cranberry Lake, main trail of 3.9 miles to state lean-to at Inlet flow, two loops at either end of 3.4 and 1.2 miles each, and 2.1 mile loop in middle; www.adirondackscenicbyways.org.

POSTWOOD PARK AND COUNT FOREST HANNAWA FALLS 4 miles south of Potsdam. The main trail starts at Postwood Park parking lot and is comprised of two loops. The first and smaller, 1.6-mile loop is located on the west side of River Road. The other loop

is located on the east side of River Road and runs for an approximate distance of 4.1 miles.

SUNY POTSDAM LEHMAN PARK 4 km. of trails off Route 56, Potsdam.

REMINGTON RECREATION TRAIL AT PARTRIDGE RUN GOLF COURSE, outer State Street, Canton, several miles of groomed trails, warm-up building.

RIVER HILL BEGINS ON SOUTH-VILLE-WEST STOCKHOLM ROAD, off Route 11B, 5 miles northeast of Potsdam. The trail's total distance is 2.3 miles and is for novice to moderate skiers.

ROBERT MOSES STATE PARK/NICANDRI NATURE CENTER, off Route 37, three miles north of Massena, 6+ miles of groomed trails, trails managed by Nicandri Nature Center; trails open dawn to dusk daily; free equipment loans at the center; **www.nicandrinaturecenter.org**.

ST. LAWRENCE GOLF/COUNTRY CLUB, off Route 11, Canton, access behind Best Western, from Pike/Russell Roads, 25 miles of groomed trails.

SWAMPER DOME LOUISVILLE ARENA TRAIL is approximately 2 miles in length running from behind the arena through the woods skirting a 90-acre meadow and back into the woods down along the Grasse River and back to the arena.

UPPER AND LOWER LAKES WILDLIFE MANAGEMENT AREA: INDIAN CREEK NATURE CENTER off Route 68 in Canton. 8 km. of trails. Several different trails at this location. **www.dec.ny.gov**.

WILSON HILL WILDLIFE MANAGEMENT AREA located in the Town of Louisville near the St. Lawrence River. From NY Route 37, turn north onto NY State Route 131 to Willard Rd. Turn north and follow the road. The parking lot will be on the left. The trail has a distance of 1.6 miles beginning at the parking area on the Willard Road. The Nature Trail divides after a short distance. The left fork heads to an observation tower, the right fork, which is the longer trail, heads westerly and ends on Wilson Hill Road.

> **Tips:**
> While playing disc golf, don't forget your cell phone and use Udisc Disc Golf App. The free downloadable provides hole maps to help navigate the course, track scores, and measure throws!

Disc Golf

SOUTH COLTON DISC GOLF COURSE is a short recreational course (10 holes) that makes good use of available trees and various natural features. Morgan Road, Colton. From Route 56 in South Colton, go north on Wind Mill Road to the 2nd right (Morgan Rd). Follow Morgan Rd. to the end and look for the sign to the first tee – a bit NE of the end of the road.

BARKEATER DISC GOLF AT OSGOOD POND weaves through a historic tree plantation that includes a lakeside front 9 and a back 9 with towering, old growth white pines. Open to the public, but on private land. Courtesy of Paul Smiths College. From the junction of State Rtes. 86 and 30, turn right onto Rte 30 and go 0.6 miles. The parking area is off the road behind some trees (east) side of the road, 50 ft north of a red gate. 1st tee is at the end of a 0.1 mile trail to the north edge of the Osgood Farm.

Both Disc Golf Courses have facebook pages.

Downhill Skiing

Skiers in Northern New York might not always want to make the trek into the Adirondack Mountains for the joy of skiing, but fortunately they don't need to. From Watertown to Plattsburgh, the North Country has several fun alpine skiing options and the region is also loaded with great groomed trails for cross-country skiing and snow boarding.

BIG BEN SKI CENTER - Seventh Street, SW, Cornwall, Ontario. (613) 933-7077 or (613) 933-3586. Located in the heart of Cornwall, Canada, "Big Ben" offers downhill skiing, snowboarding and ice skating throughout the winter months. Groups and private ski and snowboard lessons are also offered. No rental equipment available. Early in the season, Big Ben features a ski and snowboard swap day.

DRY HILL - 18160 Alpine Ridge Road, Watertown, NY. Rt. 81 to exit 44 to Rt. 232 North to Rt. 11 North to first right then second right. (315) 782-8584. **www.skidryhhill.com** This small family run ski hill in Watertown features 9 trails, 3 lifts and a fun snow tubing park. It's a great option for new skiers who can take advantage of the two hour lessons, equipment rental and lift tickets for $25.00.

GORE MOUNTAIN - North Creek, Off Rt.8 and 28, 16 miles north of Warrensburg, NY. (518) 251-2411 or 800-342-1234. **www.goremountain.com**. Gore Mountain is an alpine ski resort on Gore Mountain in the Adirondack Mountains. This ski resort has the most skiable acreage in New York. With 2,537 vertical feet, 109 trails and a snow sports school. This mountain is a popular winter destination attracting skiers from all over the North East. It is the closest large mountain in New York State to the capital metro area. Gore Mountain is one of the three ski areas owned by the State of New York and is operated by the ORDA (Olympic Regional Development Authority) a state agency. Gore Mountain has 15 lifts (nine chairlifts, 1 J-bone lift, 1 Poma lift and one magic carpet) and one snow train. Gore Mountain has a wide variety of alpine terrain catering to alpine skiers of all levels. Gore Mountain also has 12 Nordic trails of cross-country skiing.

MAPLE RIDGE SNOW PARK - 7421 East Road, Lowville, N. Y.13367 Lovely groomed trails connect to the Lewis County Fairgrounds. On site has a great warming barn that can also accommodate events. But the real draw at the Maple Ridge Snow Park is that the ski rentals are free thanks to the generous donation from the Pratt Northam Foundation.

MCCAULEY MOUNTAIN - 300 Mc Cauley Road, Old Forge, NY. (315) 369-3225. **www.oldforgeny.com**. With an altitude of 2300 ft. and a vertical drop of 633 ft. the mountain features 21 trails with difficulty levels ranging from novice to expert, two lifts and two tows. The addition of a terrain park has made McCauley increasingly popular with snowboarders. A ski school, ski shop and cozy chalet with restaurant and lounge complete the ski area package.

MOUNT PISGAH - 1 mile off Rt. 86 or Rt. 3 on Mt. Pisgah Rd, Saranac Lake, NY (518) 891-0970. **www.saranaclake.com**. Family oriented area, snow tubing park.

MOUNT TREMBLANT - 1000 Chemin des Voyageurs, Mount Tremblant, QC J8E1T1, Canada. 800-461-8711. **www.tremblant.ca**

OAK MOUNTAIN SKI CENTER - 141 Novosel Way, 1/2 mile east of Rt. 8 and Rt. 30 Speculator, NY (518) 548-3606. **www.oakmtski.com**. A three season resort for skiers, snow boarders and mountain bikers. Oak Mountain has 230 acres of skier and rider accessible terrain with the 2,400 foot mountain and a 650 vertical drop. The 13 Alpine trails are serviced by one quad and 2 T-bars. The 22 featured terrain park will entertain the family freestylers and non-skiers who can try snowboarding or tubing. Night skiing is also available.

SNOW RIDGE SKI AREA- Turin, NY South of Watertown on Rt.26. (315) 348-8456 or 800-962-8419. **www.snowridge.com**. Snow Ridge's 21 trails and terrain parks benefit from the major snow accumulation seen every year in the Tug Hill plateau and the Adirondacks. Enjoy the 22 trails and the 500 feet vertical elevation and find a run for skiers of all skill levels.

TITUS MOUNTAIN- 215 Johnson Road, Malone, NY. Six miles south of Malone on Rt. 30, then east on Fayette Road. (518) 483-3740 or 800-848-8766, **www.titusmountain.com**. Just to the north of the Adirondacks sits Titus Mountain. This is Northern New York's biggest offering for downhill skiing outside of the State Park. 50 trails, including 15 available for night skiing, 3 terrain parks, 10 lifts and 1,200 foot vertical elevation spread out over 380 acres. And to top it off, there are 2 restaurants on the mountain to fuel up at before heading for your next run.

WHITEFACE MOUNTAIN- 5021 NY 86, Wilmington, NY. (518) 946-2223 or 800-462-6263.Whiteface Mountain is the 5th highest mountain in New York State and on the peaks in the Adirondack Mountains. Set apart from most of the other High Peaks, the summit offers a 360 degree view of the Adirondacks Mountains and on a clear day Vermont and Canada. Whiteface contains 88 trails accessible by 1 gondola, 9 chairlifts and 1 conveyor lift with a 3,350 vertical drop. Some 98% of the trails are covered by snow making, excluding the glades and the slides. The slides are double-back diamond runs that are usually open at the end of the skiing season due to avalanche danger. There are between 35-40 degrees with high natural hazards (such as waterfalls, rocks, cliffs, trees and variable conditions) vertically over 1,250 feet. The slides are considered to be one of the most challenging ski slopes that are marked on a train in the Northeast.

33

Skiing in the North Country
1. Big Ben
2. Dry Hill
3. Gore Mountain
4. Maple Ridge Snow Park
5. McCauley Mountain
6. Mount Pisgah
7. Mount Tremblant
8. Oak Mountain Ski Center
9. Snow Ridge Ski Area
10. Titus Mountain
11. Whiteface Mountain

34 Drive-in Movies

FIFTY-SIX AUTO THEATRE
9783 State Highway 56, Massena
(315) 764-1250
www.jscinemas.com

BAY DRIVE-IN THEATER
RR 26, Alexandria Bay
(315) 482-3874
www.baydrivein.com

BLACK RIVER DRIVE-IN THEATRE
28035 NY-3, Black River
(315) 773-8604
www.blackriverdrivein.com

northcountrychildrensmuseum.org
10 Raymond Street, Potsdam, NY 13676
(315) 274-9380

Driving Tours

Amish Communities

Driving the back roads of the North Country, one is likely to encounter the horse-drawn black buggies of Amish residents. The Old Order Amish, descendants of the radical Anabaptist Reformation, first came to the area in 1974 in search of available farmland. St. Lawrence County is now home to three Amish communities. In the Norfolk area one finds descendants of the Swiss Amish who settled the Allen County area of Indiana. In the Heuvelton DePeyster area are Amish whose ancestors were among the early settlers of Ohio. More recently, Amish communities have developed east of Potsdam, through Hopkinton and North Lawrence. However, the most dense Amish populations are found in southern St. Lawrence County. These communities illustrate how diverse the Amish are, for they differ in a variety of ways, including the German dialect they speak at home, the style of clothing they wear, the approved haircut for boys, and the type of buggy they drive.

Amish life is rooted in agriculture , but one finds a variety of cottage industries helping supplement the income from the family farm. A drive through the county's back roads will likely lead one to the Amish farm stands offering maple syrup, fresh produce, baked goods, hand-made quilts, aprons, baskets, furniture, and storage sheds as well as firewood. The Amish welcome you to their stands but ask that you not take pictures, as that violates their religious beliefs. Also be aware that an Amish woman's pregnancy is personal and private. It is best not to remark on it. And remember, they do no business on Sundays, on Christmas, Easter or Ascension Day (40th day after Easter Sunday).

30/30 LOOP – 30 miles/30+ Amish farms
This drive starts and ends at historic Pickens Hall in Heuvelton, a general store selling a wide variety of local goods including Amish made products. It is also home to a museum and opera house.

Driving south out of Heuvelton, take the right onto Route 184, just after the bridge. Drive a short distance (2/10 mile) and then keep right to stay on Route 184. The first Amish farm is about two miles outside of Heuvelton. Broad flat fields allow you a wide view of Amish life. You may see teams of working horses plowing, harrowing, haying. Amish buggies and wagons dot the landscape, traveling to and fro. One room schoolhouses are numerous, distinguished from other buildings by the two separate outhouses that accompany them. Turn right on the West Lake Road which eventually becomes Bishop Road at the Macomb town line. Topography will change to a winding, hilly, narrow road for about three miles. At the Route 58 intersection, turn left. In about a mile and a half, turn left onto Route 184 in Pope Mills. Follow Route 184 to Kokomo Corners and turn right onto Plimpton Road into downtown DePeyster. A left turn puts you on County Route 10. Go to the stop sign and turn right onto Route 184, and head back into Heuvelton.

Alternatively, at the Macomb town line, just turn around, drive back the way you came, and see it all from the opposite direction. A beautiful, interesting ride, either way.

10/10 LOOP – 10 miles/10+ Amish farms
From Pickens General Store go up the hill and turn right across from Stewarts onto County Route 10. In about three miles bear right onto Sanderson Road. The Sanderson Road is only two miles long, but is unique in that it is without power lines and is settled only by Amish. Notice the schoolhouse at the fork. Sanderson Road ends on Route 68. Go left, then left at the blinking light in Flackville and you're back on your way into Heuvelton via County Route 10. Alternatively, Route 68 will bring you into Ogdensburg (west) or Canton (east).

Fairs, Festivals, and Events

Northern New York is full of activities, fairs, festivals and events all year long. There are many different kinds of celebrations both inside and outdoors for families to attend.

January

If you live in a place with harsh winters, one way to warm up is by having fun at a winter carnival. Winters can be brutal and carnivals help break up the monotony.

ALEXANDRIA BAY
WINTER CARNIVAL: A two-week event held in the Village of Alexandria Bay with activities including, a community snow sculpture activity, the Army Band performance, a family scavenger hunt, winter Olympics, figure skating show, basketball and volleyball contests, a movie afternoon, sledding, outdoor skating at the golf course and a bonfire with hot dogs, cocoa and s'mores. More information is available www.visit1000islands.com/alexandria-bay-winter-carnival

1000 ISLANDS POND HOCKEY CLASSIC: Hosted by the Bonnie Castle Resort, this event takes place at the Swan Bay Resort. It consists of 3 on 3 hockey with 5 co-ed divisions. For registration and additional details, visit www.riverhockeyclassic.com

COLTON
WINTERFEST: Local organizations and residents of Colton sponsor the festival held in January. Highlights of the festival include: ski races and outdoor games for the family, snowmobile races, sleigh rides, a quilt show, a flea market, spaghetti dinner, pie sale and pancake breakfast. Town website: www.townofcolton.com

LONG LAKE
LONG LAKE WINTER CARNIVAL: This weekend-long event includes cardboard sled races, snowmobile parade, coronation of the King and Queen, ice skating, wacky hat contest, balloon chase, hockey event, ladies frying pan toss, men's caber toss, live music and fireworks. For more information contact www.mylonglake.com

MASSENA
WINTER CARNIVAL:
Organized by the Greater Massena Chamber of Commerce, this event runs for 10 days and includes lots of events for families such as, a parade, fireworks, hockey competitions, a 5k walk, a moonlight ski and snowshoe, ice sculptures, geo-caching, a photo contest and kids trivia contest at the Elks Lodge. Greater Massena Chamber of Commerce office (315) 769-3525 or www.massenachamber.com

WATERTOWN
SNOWTOWN USA: Following the blizzard of 1977, Walter Cronkite actually coined the phrase "Snowtown USA" when reporting how the blizzard dumped 220 inches of snow on Watertown, NY. Through a group of volunteers, the City of Watertown's Parks and Recreation Department and the Greater Watertown-North Country Chamber of Commerce, Snowtown USA has become a 10-day celebration of the brave men and women who live in the North Country. There are several sponsored events for absolutely everyone such as a film festival, hot air balloon rides, bowling, pub crawl, snow softball, hockey games, public ice skating, sledding, pickle ball, Daniel Tiger Show, family movie night, preschool story hour, paper airplane demonstration, craft clean out night, paint and sip, Mother Goose story time, Lego club, snow art at the zoo, trivia night, and torchlight parade and fireworks. Many sponsors make this event possible.

To see a complete list of events, times and dates visit **www.snowtownusa.com**

February

ALEXANDRIA BAY
ANNUAL POLAR BEAR DIP: Join the Friends of River Hospital for one of the biggest fund raisers for River Hospital. Watch as over 100 brave individuals dive, back flip, and belly flop into the freezing St. Lawrence River, all for a wonderful cause. For more information, call River Hospital at (315) 482-1270 with any questions or visit **www.riverhospital.org**

BRASHER FALLS
TRI-TOWN WINTER FESTIVAL IN BRASHER FALLS/STOCKHOLM/WINTHROP AREA: annual mid-winter celebration in the Tri-Town area offers three days of activities throughout the area sponsored by the Tri-Town Chamber of Commerce. For a complete schedule of events go to the event's Facebook page at **www.facebook.com/groups/629946070404320**

CANTON
CANTON WINTERFEST: Organized by the Canton Chamber of Commerce, this annual community-wide event includes activities such as: snowshoeing, skiing, skating, high school and college sporting events, wine tastings, pool tournament, food, music, a craft show, an outdoor hockey tournament, and other entertainment. A complete schedule and dates can be found on the Chamber of Commerce website **www.cantonny.gov**

POLAR BEAR GOLF TOURNAMENT ST. LAWRENCE GOLF AND COUNTRY CLUB, BEST WESTERN UNIVERSITY INN: A fundraising event for the Cerebral Palsy Association features nine holes of golf in the snow, warm refreshments, prize raffles, and other outdoor activities. Those interested in participating or sponsoring should contact **www.cpnorthcountry.org**

CARTHAGE
WINTERFEST: Join in for games, horse and wagon rides, magic show, bake sale, bingo, raffle every 15 minutes, scavenger hunt, ladies frying pan toss, face painting, cardboard sled races, food, music and more. Free admission but a "Canstruction" is held to benefit the Village Ecumenical Food Pantry and Wilna-Champion Transportation Association Shuttle Bus. For more information, contact the Carthage Chamber of Commerce at (315) 493-2792.

CLAYTON
FIRE AND ICE CELEBRATION: Bundle up and step into a winter wonderland of over 25,000 pounds of ice meticulously carved into breathtaking ice sculptures, martini ice luges, and the coolest bars in town. Each year, the 1000 Islands Harbor Hotel hosts winter's hottest party, to benefit a local charity, bringing much needed merriment to winter's longest stretch. Contact the Harbor Hotel at (315) 686-1100 or **www.brownpapertickets.com**

CRANBERRY LAKE, STAR LAKE, CLIFTON FINE AND WANAKENA ADIRONDACK WHITE OUT WEEKEND: An annual winter festival with free fun for the whole family including outdoor recreation, music and arts, food, crafts, interactive presentations, kids activities, snowmobile-accessible events and much more. The full schedule of events is available at **www.sites.google.com/view/adkwow**

MASSENA
MASSENA FISHING EXPO: The premier fishing expo at the St. Lawrence Centre. They advertise the best fishing companies and brands with everything for the bass, muskie, panfish, pike, salmon, trout and walleye angler. Seminars and demonstrations are offered from industry professionals. Many top name vendors will be in attendance along with concessions. See the Facebook page for all the information **www.facebook.com/massenafishingexpo**

OGDENSBURG

RIVER SHIVER: A week-long celebration including a polar plunge into the St. Lawrence River, historic re-enactment of the Battle of Ogdensburg, public skating, Rock-N-Skate, arts and crafts, ice fishing, and other family-oriented activities. This event is organized by the Greater Ogdensburg Chamber of Commerce and serves as a fundraiser for the Chamber of Commerce and Ogdensburg Volunteer Rescue Squad. For more information visit **www.ogdensburgny.com**

REMINGTON WINE, BEER, CHEESE, CHOCOLATE AND ARTISAN FESTIVAL: Takes place at the Frederic Remington Art Museum, 303 Washington Street, Ogdensburg. This event provides a wonderful tasting and shopping experience. The website for this event is **www.fredericremington.org**

SARANAC LAKE

ADIRONDACK SNOWSHOE FEST: Activities for all levels from never shoed to experienced racers. Race at the site of the 2017 World Snowshoe Championships, held at the Dewey Mountain Recreation Center. For information, call (518) 891-4150 or check out the Adirondack Snowshoe Fest on Facebook.

BREW-SKI/FIRE AND ICE GOLF TOURNAMENT: Participants can ski or snowshoe to different brew stations set up along the beautifully maintained X-country ski trails at the Tupper Lake Cross Country Ski Center. Micro-brewers from around the region will be on hand to pour samples as you gather and mingle by the fire pits at each location. Just down the road, play golf at the Tupper Lake Country Club, sponsored by the Tupper Lake Lions Club. Check out all the information at **www.tupperlake.com**

WATERTOWN

ANNUAL NORTH COUNTRY CHILI COOK-OFF: The event will play host to more than 30 of the area's top chefs who will compete for great prizes. Admission will allow for sampling and proceeds will help fund medical transportation for local veterans and their families through the Volunteer Transportation Center. Contact (315) 755-2918 or visit the website **www.volunteertransportationcenter.org**

CABIN FEVER CRAFT FAIR: Time to get out of the house and attend one of the first craft fairs of the year at the Ramada Inn. For information, call (315) 777-1495

MARCH

CAPE VINCENT

WINTER-GREEN VOLLEYBALL TOURNAMENT: This event takes place in downtown Cape Vincent. Featuring music, firepits, hot cocoa and a cash prize for the winning team. Contact the Cape Vincent Chamber of Commerce at (315) 654-2481.

LAKE PLACID

ANNUAL LAKE PLACID LOPPET AND KORT LOPPET: taking place at Mt. Van Hoevenberg Olympic Venue, this event is one of the most challenging citizen races in the world. This is the perfect race for recreational to expert skiers who are looking for a unique and challenging race. Everyone who crosses the finish line wins a prize. For more information, visit **www.adirondack.net**

OGDENSBURG

OGDENSBURG EXPO AT THE GOLDEN DOME: the major fundraiser for the Ogdensburg Boys and Girls Club. Usually held in March, the weekend features all types of exhibits (cars, boats, crafts, products, etc) as well as concessions, carnival games and entertainment. For information, to volunteer or participate, contact: (315) 393-1241 or email: obgc@hotmail.com

ST. LAWRENCE COUNTY MAPLE WEEKENDS: Participating producers open their sugar shacks for tours and demonstrations. Part of New York State Maple Weekend. Look alphabetically under Maple in this book.

APRIL

CANTON
PETER RABBIT IN THE PARK FEST: Hosted by the Canton Chamber of Commerce, this festival takes place at the Canton Pavilion with an annual Easter Egg Hunt for ages 6 and younger, games, face painting, a cake walk, bowling, coloring, and other Easter-themed activities. For more information call: (315) 386-8255 or email: cantonchamberny@gmail.com

CLAYTON
1000 ISLANDS SPRING BOAT SHOW: Held at Cerow Recreation Park Arena, featuring runabouts, fishing boats, pontoons, docks, lifts, personal watercraft marine insurance and much more with numerous exhibitors, concessions and a raffle. For a complete list of exhibits, dates and times contact the Clayton Chamber of Commerce at (315) 686-3771.

MASSENA
SPORTSMEN'S EXPO: The Massena Rod And Gun Club sponsors this event, held in the Massena Arena. The weekend includes firearms for sale from major gun vendors, and sellers offering gear, clothing and equipment for hunting, archery, camping, boating, trapping and fishing. Also, recreational vehicles will be on display and the Rod and Gun Club will be selling concessions. For more information, contact the club at (315) 769-3205 or visit their Facebook page at Rod-Gun Club Massena.

OGDENSBURG
SPORTSMEN'S SHOW: A one-day event sponsored by the Ogdensburg Chamber of Commerce held at the Ogdensburg Golden Dome featuring a huge rifle raffle, taxidermy demos and displays, fishing, hunting, trapping vendors, boats, ATV's and much more. For more information contact the Ogdensburg Chamber of Commerce at (315) 393-3620 or info@ **www.ogdensburgny.com**

POTSDAM
THE REALLY BIG SHOW: St. Lawrence County Chamber of Commerce's Home, Garden, and Business Show. The Show runs from Friday afternoon through Saturday at Cheel Arena on Clarkson University. The Really Big Show is a combination event that caters to the ready-for-spring public as well as to business. It allows regional businesses and organizations of all sizes and types to promote products and services, sell products, and build relationships with other professionals for future business growth. Local and area food, wine and craft vendors will also be on hand showcasing goods. Contact the St. Lawrence County Chamber of Commerce at (315) 386-4000 or jroberts@stlawrencecountychamber.org

WATERTOWN
ANNUAL ANTIQUE SHOW AND SALE: A two-day event held at the Dulles State Office Building to benefit the Credo Community Center Foundation. For information call (315) 788-1530.

MAY

ALEXANDRIA BAY
BLESSING OF THE FLEET: A community effort to bless the fleet of seagoing vessels and their crews for safe passage and prosperity. A tradition in Alexandria Bay since 1977. For more information contact the Alexandria Bay Chamber of Commerce at (315) 482-9531 or info@alexbay.org

CANTON
CANOE WEEKEND: One of the state's premier canoe races with Rushton, C-1, C-2, professional point and recreational races sponsored by St. Lawrence Valley Paddlers. Canton was home to John Henry Rushton and his famous boatworks, founded in 1875. In his honor, this historic event began in 1962 and was originally known as the "Rushton Memorial Canoe Race". The event has continued to grow and has become known for its prestigious pro race. Today, pro, amateur, and recreational races all remain a part of the weekend line up. Both the pro and amateur races are official events in the sport of marathon canoe racing. For more information, pictures and great videos, visit the event website: **www.cantoncanoeweekend.org**

JUNE

ALEXANDRIA BAY
ANNUAL TI RIVER RUN: A motorcycle event featuring live music, bike builders, vendors, loud pipes contest, custom bike show, poker run and tattoo contest. For more information and dates call (315) 771-1435.

CANTON
ST. LAWRENCE COUNTY DAIRY PRINCESS FESTIVAL: The festival is usually held on the first weekend of June and involves a big parade and events in the Village Park. Events include "big wheel" races, frog jumping contest, live music, dairy displays, cake walk, crafts, chicken barbecue and concessions. For more information, contact the Canton Chamber of Commerce at (315) 386-8255 or www.cantonny.gov

CLAYTON
GREAT NEW YORK STATE FOOD AND WINE FESTIVAL: This is an event celebrating quality "Made in New York" food and wine products including candy, cheese, meat, nuts, dips and sauces, herbs and spices, maple products, cookies, fudge, desserts, soda, coffee, jerky, popcorn, wine flour, distilled spirits and of course New York State wines. Over 70 exhibitors anxious to introduce their great products to sample and purchase. This fun, family-friendly festival in the largest of its kind in the area. Sponsored ny the Clayton Chamber of Commerce, call (315) 686-3771 or visit info@1000islands-clayton.com

LAKE PLACID
LAKE PLACID MARATHON AND HALF: A premier early season race that is certified and a qualifier for the Boston Marathon. Offers both a full and half marathons with athlete food and aid stations. For all the details and descriptions visit www.LakePlacidMarathon.com

MADRID
MADRID CANOE REGATTA: The Madrid Canoe Regatta is a series of races held annually over two days in early June on the Grasse River at Madrid Municipal Park, including recreational, amateur, pro and marathon races. Camping is available on-site free of charge. For information, check the race web page www.slvpaddlers.org. There is email information on the website.

ANNUAL SPRING ANTIQUE GAS AND STEAM ENGINE EXHIBITION: Held at the St. Lawrence Power and Equipment Museum, 1755 State Highway 345, Madrid. This is an exhibition of antique engines and tractors with tractor pull contests. For more information see the website www.slpowermuseum.com

OGDENSBURG
CAR-B-QUE: A combination Barbeque and Cruise-in, along with a fun filled day of entertainment, featuring vendors, music, raffles, and much more, sponsored by the Ogdensburg Chamber of Commerce. Held on the grounds of the Dobisky Visitor's Center in Ogdensburg. For more information contact the Ogdensburg Chamber of Commerce at www.ogdensburgny.com

PAUL SMITHS
ADIRONDACK BOREAL BIRDING FESTIVAL: A 3-day Adirondack birding festival held at Paul Smith's College Visitors Interpretive Center.

Offers day-long birding workshops across the Adirondack region with a speaker and artisan market. For more information, call (518) 327-6241 or visit **www.paulsmiths.edu**

TUPPER LAKE
ANNUAL TINMAN TRIATHLON: Tupper Lake is home to one of the longest-running triathlons in the United States. Originally started in 1983, this race takes place in the beautiful Adirondack Mountains. For more information for both racers and spectators, visit **www.tupperlake.com**

ANNUAL WARRIOR RUN: An obstacle race through mud, field, and crazy Adirondack terrain. Participants will start at Raquette River Brewing in downtown Tupper Lake and spectators will be able to watch along the trail. Enjoy an afternoon of live music, good food and great craft beer. Check out the website **www.tupperlake.com/warriorrun**

JULY

ALEXANDRIA BAY
INDEPENDENCE DAY FIREWORKS: An amazing show over Boldt Castle that begins at dusk. More information available at the Alexandria Bay Chamber of Commerce (315) 482-9531 or info@alexbay.org

BUSKERS IN THE BAY: Street performers are hosted on Market Street in Alex Bay. For more information and a complete list of performers contact the Alex Bay Chamber of Commerce at (315) 482-9531 or info@alexbay.org

SUMMER CRAFT FAIR: Held at the Scenic View Park Pavilion located at 8 Fuller Street. For additional details, contact the Alexandria Bay Chamber of Commerce at (315) 482-9531 or **www.visitalexbay.org**

CAPE VINCENT
FRENCH FESTIVAL: A huge annual French weekend celebration featuring a family block dance, pancake breakfast, French pastries, artisan and craft fair, children's puppet show, children's games and amusements, street entertainers, live music, a huge parade, a French mass, and fireworks at the waterfront. For information, call (315) 654-2481 or visit **www.capevincent.org**

CLAYTON
ANNUAL 1000 ISLANDS POKER RUN: A grassroots, volunteer-driven event, dedicated to the charitable needs and economic development of the Thousand Islands region. The goal of the run is to host events that promote the local river communities and preserve the historic integrity of the Thousand Islands. This promises to be an exciting event with spectacular boats in a family-friendly environment with 100% of the profits going to charity. For more information and dates, contact **www.1000islandsrun.com**

INDEPENDENCE DAY FIREWORKS DISPLAY: The improved display is set off in front of Calumet Island and is viewable from the waterfront (Riverside Drive). Donations are greatly appreciated and checks can be made out to the Clayton Chamber of Commerce.

DECOY AND WILDLIFE ART SHOW: This annual event is put on by the Thousand Islands Museum. Featuring decoy carvers, wildlife artwork, duck calls, and collectibles with many other activities and exhibitions. This is the major fundraiser for the Thousand Islands Museum. The number to call for more information is (315) 686-5794 or visit **www.timuseum.org**

ANTIQUE BOAT SHOW: Located in the 1000 Islands on the St. Lawrence River, the Antique Boat Museum is the premier freshwater boating museum in North America. The museum holds over 300 unique boats and hosts the longest running annual boat show. The 4.5 acre campus is located at 750 Mary Street in Clayton. To contact the museum, call (315) 686-4104 or fax (315) 686-2775.

COLTON
COLTON COUNTRY DAYS: Colton Country Days showcases a variety of things to see and do around the town with events scheduled throughout the week which celebrate the community with music, art, food, frog jumping contests, dramatic productions, and barn quilts. Many of the events are free. Check the complete schedule posted on the Town of Colton's website **www.townofcolton.com**

MADRID
CIVIL WAR REENACTMENT WEEKEND: A collaboration of the St. Lawrence County Historical Association and the St. Lawrence Power and Equipment Museum in Madrid. The museum is currently working to add a Civil War-era fort to its display of power and steam engines. Contact **www.slpowermuseum.com**

MASSENA
MASSENA BLOCK DANCE AND CAR SHOW: Classic cars, trucks, and motorcycles on display at the St. Lawrence Centre mall. Also look for live entertainment, raffles, and face painting. For exact dates go to **www.stlawrencecentre.com**

POTSDAM
POTSDAM SUMMER FESTIVAL: Sidewalk sales, ice cream social, bounce houses, 5K walk/run, street music, book sale, craft sale and antique car show in Ives Park, and fireworks take place all over Potsdam. Market Street is closed and a large stage erected for the continuous live music. One of the highlights is the Potsdam Fire Department Parade and Run to the River. This event occurs concurrently with the alumni reunions of Clarkson University and SUNY Potsdam and is sponsored by the Potsdam Chamber of Commerce and usually takes place the weekend after July 4th. For exact dates and listing of activities **www.potsdamchamber.com**

OGDENSBURG
OGDENSBURG INTERNATIONAL SEAWAY FESTIVAL: A 10 day event that includes a children's fishing derby, a huge fireworks display, parade, wine and craft show at Lockwood Arena, amusement rides, live music, Founder's Weekend with Reenactments of the French and Indian war battles, High School Battle of the Bands, and a talent competition. This event draws thousands of people from all over the North Country and Canada and is sponsored by many local corporations and the Greater Ogdensburg Chamber of Commerce. A complete list of events can be found at **www.ogdensburgseawayfestival.org**

SACKETS HARBOR
CAN-AM FESTIVAL: The Can-Am Festival is a celebration of the friendship and shared lake heritage of the United States and Canada and features one of the North Country's largest parades. Also included in the weekend event are live music, soapbox races, craft and food vendors, children's entertainment and activities, farmer's market, wine garden, shootout lacrosse tournament, plein air festival and silent auction, and bake sale. To learn more call (315) 646-6070

TUPPER LAKE
TUPPER LAKE WOODSMEN'S DAYS: A weekend-long festival designed to celebrate the region's heritage of logging and lumberjacking. Presented by the Tupper Lake Woodsmen's Association, the annual event has something for everyone, including heavy equipment demonstrations and competitions, chainsaw carving competitions, lumberjack shows, night games (including Tug-of-War and the infamous Greased Pole Climb), chil-

dren's activities, a gala parade, and much more. For a complete schedule of events and more information, visit **www.tupperlake.com**

WATERTOWN
JEFFERSON COUNTY FAIR: The longest continuously operating fair in the United States! You will find a midway with amusement rides, food and creative craft judging, art judging, a scarecrow contest and a variety of animal judging exhibits, demonstrations and husbandry lessons. There is also live music, a demolition derby, fire safety exhibits, and many vendors and concessions available. There are many sponsors for this event and information can be found on the website **www.jeffcofair.org**

AUGUST

ALEXANDRIA BAY
BILL JONHSTON'S PIRATE DAYS: 10 days filled with family fun and special events, this event commemorates some of the exploits of Bill Johnston. Pirate ships attack the village from the St. Lawrence River as the villagers try to stave them off. You are invited to join in the spirit by dressing up as a Pirate, Patriot or Indian. Most events are free and a complete list is available from the Alexandria Bay Chamber of Commerce at (315) 482-9531 or **www.visitalexbay.org**

ROCKIN' THE BAY: A classic rock and classic cars weekend. Features a classic rock and roll block dance and classic car rally and DJ. For specific information and dates, contact the Alexandria Bay Chamber of Commerce at (315) 482-9531 or **www.visitalexbay.org**

GOUVERNEUR/ST. LAWRENCE COUNTY FAIR: A week-long county fair with a variety of events including live music and concerts, a fireman's parade, livestock competitions and exhibits, amusement rides, games, demonstrations, concessions, harness racing, high school band competitions, talent show, demolition derby, professional tough trucks, and much more. Contact (315) 771-7690 or go to the fair website **www.gouverneurfair.net**

MALONE
FRANKLIN COUNTY FAIR: A safe, family-friendly environment filled with rides and games as well as events and exhibits which continue to honor the history of agriculture in the area. There is plenty to do during this week-long event including activities such as a demolition derby, legendary rock bands, animal and livestock exhibitions, craft exhibitions, amusement rides, food vendors, horse racing and a demolition derby. For specifics, call (518) 483-0721 or visit info@frcofair.com

OGDENSBURG
TASTE OF THE NORTH COUNTRY FESTIVAL: the Greater Ogdensburg Chamber of Commerce and the City of Ogdensburg are sponsors of this signature event of the summer, formerly known as the Wine, Beer and Food Festival. New York State wines are available for sampling and purchasing at the Lockwood Civic Center. Food cooking demonstrations and local artisans also round out the program. More information is available at **www.ogdensburgny.com/events/wine-beer-food-festival**

WADDINGTON
WADDINGTON HOMECOMING: Features live music, entertainment, food and carnival games, a pet show, parade, carnival games, community picnic, bed races, a lip synch contest and fireworks. Check out he event on Facebook **www.facebook.com/WaddingtonHomecoming**

SEPTEMBER

ALEXANDRIA BAY
BLUES IN THE BAY: Held on Labor Day weekend, this is 4 days of free blues music, combined with a craft fair at Scenic View Park Pavilion. For a complete list of participating bands, call (315) 482-9531 or visit **www.visitalexbay.org/events/blues-in-the-bay**

ROLLIN' STREET THUNDER: A "hogs and rods" show located on Market Street. Classic cars and motorcycles are welcome with 50's and 60's music. Sponsored by the Alexandria Bay Chamber of Commerce. For more information call (315) 482-9531 or visit www.visitalexbay.org/events/rollin-street-thunder

ALEX BAY WINE FESTIVAL AND FARMER'S MARKET: Enjoy your tastings overlooking the beautiful St. Lawrence River and iconic Boldt Castle, held at the Scenic View Park Pavilion. For more information call the Chamber at (315) 482-9531 or visit www.visit.alexbay.org/annual-alex-bay-events/alex-bay-wine-festival-farmers-market

MADRID
ANNUAL OLD FASHIONED HARVEST DAYS EXHIBITION: Held at the St. Lawrence Power and Equipment Museum, usually at the end of August or beginning of September. The event includes exhibits of antique cars, tractors, trucks, horse and tractor pulls, working antique engines, 1850's one-room school house and log cabin, show repair shop, carriage barn, maple sugar house, farm animals, 1920's gas station, blacksmith, print shop, collection building, wagon rides, horse and tractor parades, early textile demonstrations, flea market, raffles, ice cream, kids pedal tractor pull and races, baked goods, ice cream and great food all weekend. The website is www.slpowermuseum.com

CAPE VINCENT
AUTOS ON THE RIVER: An annual vintage and classic car show held on Labor Day weekend. Contact the Cape Vincent Chamber of Commerce for more information (315) 654-2481

OKTOBERFEST: Featuring German music, dancers, food, beer and wine in downtown Cape Vincent. Look for live German performers and German food sold by the Cape Vincent Fire Department, biergarten, sampler mugs, beer stein races, and lederhosen and dirndl contests. Sponsored by the Cape Vincent Chamber of Commerce, call (315) 654-2481 for more information.

MALONE
HARVEST FEST AND CIVIL WAR LIVING HISTORY: Adirondack Regiment of Civil War Re-enactors will be at the Wilder Farm, located just outside of Malone. Featuring living history with displays, vignettes and skirmishes as well as craft and farm market vendors, music, life skills demonstrations, 19th century games and kids activities, self-guided tours of the Wilder farm and food. Contact the Malone Chamber of Commerce at (518) 483-1207 or visit www.visitmalone.com

MASSENA
HARVEST FESTIVAL: The greater Massena Chamber of Commerce celebrates Harvest Festival with a day full of scarecrow making, wagon rides, food and music. Several streets in the downtown area will be blocked off to make room for activities such as face painting, pumpkin painting, dance demonstrations, horse-drawn wagon rides, displays, game booths, kid's crafts. Many vendors are on hand to provide information, demonstrations and items for sale. For more information visit www.massenachamber.com

RENSSELAER FALLS
REMINGTON II CANOE RACES: A six mile downstream race on the Oswegatchie River from Rensselaer Falls to Heuvelton, New York. The course is primarily flatwater, however there are two short sets of Class 1 rapids which may be run or portaged depending on the water level. For more information, check www.slvpaddlers.org

WATERTOWN
BLACK RIVER FALL FEST: Held in downtown Watertown on Public Square, this event features many craft and food vendors, a car show, concessions, live music, wine tasting and demonstrations. This is a family-friendly event, sponsored by the Downtown Business Association, is free to attend.

OCTOBER

ALEXANDRIA BAY
HALLOWEEN FESTIVAL: Trick-or-treating with the local businesses, hayrides, crafts, ghost tours, a costume contest and more, located at Scenic View Park Pavilion on Fuller Street. Sponsored by the Alexandria Bay Chamber of Commerce (315) 482-9531.

CANTON
PHANTOMS IN THE PARK: This annual event, co-sponsored by the Canton Chamber of Commerce, St. Lawrence University and SUNY Canton, features a Halloween parade, costume contest, Halloween games, pumpkin decorating, and trick-or-treating at area businesses. Both colleges set up a variety of contests for the children as well. For more information contact the Canton Chamber of Commerce **www.cantonny.gov**

REMINGTON ARTS FESTIVAL: A celebration of Arts and Arts Excellence in the North Country. Features include an art show and sale as well as horse-drawn carriage tours of downtown Canton. Check out **www.facebook.com/RemingtonArtsFestival**

CLAYTON
PUNKIN CHUNKIN: Come watch local teams of adults and kids compete to see who can catapult a pumpkin the farthest into the St. Lawrence River. The home-built trebuchets will be set up in Frink Park in downtown Clayton. Also look for a barbecue, bounce houses and numerous vendors. Hosted by the Clayton Chamber of Commerce, who can be reached at (315) 686-3771 or visit info@1000islands-clayton.com

OGTORERFEST: An annual event that celebrates Ogdensburg with a German Oktoberfest feel. They have local vendors, a beer garden, food and raffles. This event is sponsored by the Greater Ogdensburg Chamber of Commerce and takes place at the Lockwood Civic Center, 141 East River Street. More information can be found on the Chamber of Commerce website **www.ogdensburgny.com/events/ogtoberfest**

POTSDAM
FRIGHT NIGHT: A family friendly event sponsored by the Potsdam Chamber of Commerce. Takes place downtown in the early evening a few days before Halloween. There are vendors, activities, food, candy, a bonfire, fire truck rides and late night shopping. Prizes are awarded for the best Halloween costumes in several categories. Visit the Potsdam Chamber website **www.potsdamchamber.com** or check out the Facebook page **www.facebook.com/events/potsdam-chamber-of-commerce**

NOVEMBER

ACROSS ST. LAWRENCE COUNTY
ARTISTS' STUDIO TOUR: The tour offers community residents and visitors the opportunity to take a self-guided driving tour of over a dozen artists' workspaces. **www.slcartscouncil.org**

OGDENSBURG
LIGHT UP THE NIGHT PARADE: Annual event in Ogdensburg that is coordinated by the Lions Club. There are lighted floats, vehicles, and marching groups to welcome Santa and Mrs. Claus to ring in the holiday season. Check the website for dates and times **www.ogdensburgny.com**

POTSDAM
CRAFT, FOOD, AND WINE SHOW: Sponsored by the St. Lawrence County Chamber of Commerce, this show usually takes place at Cheel Arena located on the Clarkson University campus. More than 100 vendors and local artisans sell hand-crafted or homemade products, including food, jewelry, furniture, quilts, photography, artwork, wine, and more. There is something for everyone and a great way to support local businesses. One of the best craft fairs in the county! This event is held in the Clarkson University hockey arena, therefore, the dates change each year according to the hockey

schedule. For more information and dates, contact the St. Lawrence County Chamber of Commerce at (315) 386-4000 or www.VisitSTLC.com

DECEMBER

LISBON
LIGHTS ON THE RIVER:
Annual holiday festival of lights and displays on the St. Lawrence River, with proceeds going to local food pantries. As many as 75 light displays made by local businesses and families at the Lisbon Beach. Free but donations are welcomed. See the website
www.lightsontheriver.org

THE EMPIRE STATE WINTER GAMES is a multi-day sports event hosted in New York State's Adirondacks at the end of January and the beginning of February. The games bring together athletes from across the state to compete in over 30 winter sports events. You do not have to be a New York State resident to participate in the Empire State Games and most sports are open to all levels. Sports venues are located in Lake Placid, Wilmington, Saranac Lake, Tupper Lake, Malone and Paul Smiths. Sports included are: alpine skiing, adaptive alpine, biathlon, adaptive biathlon, bobsled, adaptive bobsled, cross country skiing, figure skating, freestyle moguls, luge, Nordic combined, skeleton, skicross, adaptive skicross, ski jumping, ski orienteering, snowboard cross, adaptive snowcross, snowshoe, speed skating, squirt hockey, winter bike, hockey, adaptive hockey, and esports. For information, visit
www.empirestatewintergames.com

Lake Placid, New York gained international fame as host of the 1932 and 1980 Winter Olympic Games. Even decades after these two epic events, the region honors its Olympic heritage as a training ground for each new generation of athletes. Several Olympic venues are open to visitors, including the ski jumping complex and the bobsled run at Mt. Van Hoevenberg, the speed skating oval on Main Street, and the ice rinks inside the Herb Brooks Arena. Many training events, qualifiers, and competitions are held at these venues every year. Some events are biennial or held sporadically. For more information about available events, dates, times maps and all information, contact
www.lakeplacid.com
www.lakeplacidskating.com
www.whiteface.com
www.adirondack.net

Olympic Sites Passport is perfect for someone planning a visit to the area, giving you access to several activities at the Lake Placid Olympic Site for a bundled price of just $40. These are available for purchase online or at venues. Not all events and sites are available on a daily basis. Be sure to check the Activities and Events Calendar, located at
www.whiteface.com

SARANAC LAKE WINTER CARNIVAL:
This is one of the oldest winter carnivals in the United States! This grassroots, volunteer driven festival has been celebrating the cold since 1897 with many events that center around a massive ice palace that measures 60 feet high which is open for visitors to explore. The 10 day themed carnival also includes an icicle contest, snow rugby, snowshoe softball, fireman's broomball, skiing, skating, ultimate Frisbee games, Arctic golf, and lots more. It ends with a gala parade and huge fireworks finale. This is one of the premier events in New York State – not to be missed! For more information about the carnival, visit a website dedicated to the Ice Carnival telling Ice Palace construction details, a history of the Festival and a complete schedule of activities.
www.saranaclakewintercarnival.com

Fishing

Few areas in New York State can rival the variety of fishing opportunities in Northern New York. The North Country is truly a "country for all seasons" and a "country for all anglers". Consider the possibilities for muskies in Massena, ice fishing for yellow perch and northern pike in Chippewa Bay, jiggling for walleye on the Racquette River reservoirs, canoeing for small mouth bass on the Grasse River, fly fishing for brown trout on the St. Regis River, small boating for lake trout at Trout Lake and rainbows at Star Lake. Additionally, trolling for trophy brook trout at Cranberrry Lake, jigging for black crappies and casting for large mouth bass at Black Lake and hiking the wilderness for native brook front swims for casting about a 12 foot pole to fight with a mighty carp. North Country fishing is legendary. Clear fast streams, rocky shoreline and plenty of tricky hiding spots are sure signs you are in casting country.

Fish Lake Ontario, the big water, for trout, salmon and walleye or head over into the river system for pike, bass and panfish. The protected bays are prime fishing spots; tributaries like the Black River offer great off season casting opportunities.

Brook, brown and rainbow trout abound in rivers of the north. In addition, opportunities exist for landlocked salmon, smallmouth bass, and walleyes. Wading or canoeing are the primary means of accessing fish, but anglers can also fish from the shore, a small boat, or even a whitewater raft. While most fishers wade or fish from a specific site and then return to that spot, two other options exist. One is to use two vehicles and wade or canoe from the put-in to the take-out spot. On Point A to Point B outings, canoeists have the option of paddling in flat-water stretches and then wading in riffle areas. A second option, requiring just a single vehicle, is for waders to work with a partner. Each begins at a different location and the two anglers fish towards each other and pass at mid-point in the venture.

Early season is a good time to fish rivers. Populations are high due to fresh stockings and holdover trout, and the fish have not seen a lot of artificial yet. During the summer months, the most productive times are from 5:30 to 8:30 a.m. and the last hour before sunset. Pocket water offers the best chance for larger trout in mid-summer.

Fishing pressure drops off once school begins in September. At the same time, water temperature drops, flows generally increase, and big-fly hatches occur, all of which translates into first-rate fishing. Among the top brown trout waters are Brant Lake, Indian Lake, Lake Bonaparte, Lake Colby, Lake Eaton, Lake Pleasant, Lewey Lake, Scanadaga Lake, Thirteenth Lake and Upper Saranac Lake.

In spring and fall, anglers catch rainbow trout throughout the day, but summer fishers have their best luck in the early morning and evening. Trolling flashy artificials in the evening is particularly popular. Summer anglers also chum with corn for action after sunset. Fly fishers have success using black leeches and dark woody buggers. Prime rainbow trout holding locations include river mouths, necked down areas between islands, and shoreline drop-offs.

Many north waters are heavily stocked with rainbow trout. The top-ranked waters for rainbows near their annual stockings are: Brant Lake (11,500), Chazy Lake (24,500), Eighth Lake (5,700), Glen Lake (4,600), Lake Colby (3,400), Lake Eaton (2,000), Lake Placid (8,450), Lake Pleasant (12,000), Paradox Lake (7,600), Sacandaga Lake (12,000), Seventh Lake (12,300), Upper Chateaugay Lake (4,500), and Upper Saranac Lake (5,600).

Lake trout thrive in many Adirondack waters because of the cool water temperatures and an abundance of baitfish. Two keys to catching lakers are finding water temperatures in the 48 to 52 degree range and then presenting slow-moving offerings close to bottom. In the spring, look for lake trout among drop-offs, near points, and on rocky shoals. In summer, lake trout inhabit deep water near schools of baitfish, and in autumn they head to rocky shoals for spawning. The best shoals have adjacent deep water. Trolling is the preferred technique, and summer requires the use of downriggers, diving devices, or weights to get offerings to the fish. A number of anglers take lakers by hand jigging spoons on wire line or fishing baitfish on bottom.

Some lakes have a reputation for producing high numbers of small to medium size trout, but biologists believe several lakes are capable of producing a New York State record lake trout. The sixteen top ranked lakes are: Blue Mountain Lake, Chazy Lake, Eighth Lake, Indian Lake, Lake Eaton, Lake Lila (300-yard carry required), Lake Placid, Paradox Lake, Piseco Lake, Raquette Lake, Schroon Lake, Seventh Lake, Taylor Pond, Tupper Lake, Upper Saranac Lake and Upper Chateaugay Lake.

ST. LAWRENCE RIVER

The St. Lawrence River forms the northern boundary of the county, state and the U.S. The scenery alone makes any outing a memorable experience. This powerful flow offers first-rate angling for muskies, walleyes, northern pike, smallmouth bass, and panfish along its entire length.

BLACK LAKE

The largest of the Indian River lakes, Black Lake has 20 mile length and 60 miles of shoreline. A fisheries biologist once referred to the lake as a "fish factory". Indeed, this water does hold incredible populations of gamefish and panfish. A number of national publications have rated Black Lake among the ten best bass waters in the country. The lake's crappie marathons and outstanding ice fishing also contribute to its fine reputation: a fisherman's paradise. Black Lake is one the most widely known fishing and vacations spots in New York State. Thousands of anglers, both young and old, travel to the shores of Black Lake each year. While some anglers are busy filling their coolers with perch, bluegill and crappie, others are challenged to land trophy size northern pike in the 10 to 12 pound range. Largemouth bass to 7 pounds and smallmouth bass to 5 pounds are not uncommon here. Walleye and huge catfish are plentiful and even an occasional monster muskie is landed. For more information, call or write: The Black Lake Chamber of Commerce, 2692 County Rt. 6, Hammond, NY 13646. (315) 375-8640. blcc@blacklake.org. or www.blacklake.org.

OSWEGATCHIE RIVER

Meandering through St. Lawrence County from Newton Falls to Ogdensburg where it empties into the St. Lawrence River, the Oswegatchie River offers anglers 100 miles of fishable water. Nearly 40 public access sites dot the river. Good fishing exists for shore anglers, waders, and boaters who use canoes, car-top boats, or small trailered boats. Available species include smallmouth bass, walleye, northern pike, catfish, some largemouth bass, and the occasional muskie.

The headwaters of the Oswegatchie River above High Falls might be the county's best spot for fishing native brook trout in a remote setting. Accessible by a 13.5 mile canoe trip from Inlet and a portage around High Falls, this stretch of river teems with native brookies albeit small ones.

GRASSE RIVER

The Grasse River for the most part, receives light angling pressure. Smallmouth bass, walleyes, and panfish can be found throughout most of the middle and lower stretches of the Grasse. Some sections hold northern pike and even muskies.

PLUMB BROOK

The Grasse River and Plumb Brook rate highly for brown trout. Annual stockings of browns include nearly 700 in the South Branch of the Grasse in the town of Clare, over 2,000 in the Grasse River in the Town of Russell, and over 4,000 in Plumb Brook in the Town of Russell.

RACQUETTE RIVER AND RESERVOIRS

From the mouth of the river to the dam at Colton Flow, the Racquette is typical of other small rivers that flow through the county. Access is available at numerous points, fishing pressure is light, and gamefish range from crappies to muskies on the lower sections to trout on the upper regions. The construction of hydroelectric dams on the Racquette River created a series of eight reservoirs: Upper Impoundments, Carry Falls, Stark Falls, Blake Falls, Rainbow Falls, South Colton, Higley Flow, and Colton Flow. These reservoirs are found along a 30 mile stretch of river.

LAKE OZONIA - ST. REGIS RIVER

Special regulations allow year round fishing at this popular lake which receives annual DEC stockings of rainbow trout and splake numbering 5,000. In recent years, Lake Ozonia has also been stocked with lake trout, land-locked salmon, and brown trout. The browns are two year old trout measuring 15 inches. The high numbers of trout overshadow the outstanding yellow perch fishing that exists. The St. Regis River ranks among the county's most popular trout streams. Special regulations also allow year round fishing on the St. Regis between Fort Jackson and Mill Street in the town of Hopkinton.

MOON LAKE - WOLF LAKE

The 4,316 acre Wolf Lake State Forest by Trout Lake offers a unique opportunity for anglers who are willing to carry a canoe along a wooded trail to Wolf and Moon Lakes. Largemouth bass are found in these backwoods ponds that see few visitors.

TROUT LAKE - SYLVIA LAKE

Trout Lake has a reputation for offering quality rainbow trout and lake trout fishing. Sylvia Lake resembles Trout Lake in several ways. Both are deep water lakes, both hold populations of rainbows and lakers, and both see early ice out because of low elevations.

Fishing Licenses

Fishing licenses are available at most town municipal offices throughout the State Department of Environmental Conservation, some local sports stores and recreation stores or by calling 1-800-933-2257.

The following are the license fees for state residents and non-residents:

	RESIDENTS	NON-RESIDENTS
FISHING	$25 (AGES 16-69)	$50
ONE DAY FISHING	$5	$10
SEVEN DAY FISHING	$12	
SENIOR	(70+) $5	

Please note that prices may vary.

CRANBERRY LAKE - FIVE PONDS WILDERNESS AREA - STAR LAKE

Anglers will find three types of fishing at Cranberry Lake: open water fishing on the lake itself, stream fishing at the Oswegatchie River outlet, and the Five Ponds Wilderness Area where brook trout lurk in the backwoods ponds. Star Lake is stocked with rainbow, brown and lake trout with canoe access by a short carry.

MASSAWEPIE AREA

Massawepie Lake, Long Pond, Deer Pond, The Town Line Pond, and Pine Pond offer Adirondack trout fishing opportunities. Except for Pine Pond, which requires a paddle across the lower end of the Massawepie Lake, the waters have roadside access. In 1992, Canton angler Rick Mace set the New York State brook trout record by landing a 21inch, 4 pound 13 ounce brookies at Deer Pond.

OTHER AREAS FOR GREAT FISHING

HARRIS LAKE
Harris Lake has decent numbers of smallmouth and largemouth bass as well as some northern pike. Rocky areas hold smallies while weedy areas hold large mouths and northern. Access from the ramp at the state campground.

LONG LAKE
The best smallmouth bass fishing is found in the northern section of the lake near the islands. Two good pike spots are the shallow, weedy areas at Big Brook Bay and at the lake's outlet in the northeast corner. The southern section of the lake has a growing largemouth bass fishery with the possibility of anglers catching a five pound bucketmouth. DEC maintains a launch in the Village of Long Lake.

FISHING IN THE SEAWAY VALLEY
(613) 938-4748 or 800-937-4748
www.cornwalltourism.com
The St. Lawrence River and Lake St. Francis offer excellent fishing for perch, walleye and small mouth and large mouth bass. Try your luck by boat or from the shoreline, or consider using the services of a professional fishing and hunting guide.

KEVIN WHITE'S CANADIAN ST. LAWRENCE CARP FISHING SCHOOL
(613) 543-0600
www.canadiancarpfishing.com
The St. Lawrence River is a place to go carp fishing. Kevin White's Carp Fishing offers carp fishing clinics, UK tackle, a professional UK guide, bait and transportation and Bed & Breakfast Packages.

THE FISHING HUT
(613) 933-4636 www.fishinghut.ca
The "Hut" is centrally located in Cornwall and carries a variety of supplies for all fishing and hunting enthusiasts. Fishing, ice fishing, fly fishing or hunting tackle equipment and accessories, camping and boating equipment, live bait, live trap cages, smokers, underwater cameras and Shimano rods and reels. If it has something to do with fishing or hunting they have it or have access to it. Residential and non-residential Ontario hunting and fishing licenses are sold on the premises.

Fishing Guides

All New York State Fishing Guides must be licensed by the Department of Environmental Conservation. A list of fishing guides is available at the Department of Environment Conservation offices. New York State Outdoor Guide Association (NYSOGA) provides free Guides to Licensed Guides of New York State at 866-469-7642 or at wwwnysoga.com.

FISHING CHARTERS/GUIDES

- Patrick Simpson, Alexandria Bay (315) 482-4503/(315) 783-6088; pjscshipmotel.com
- Allen Benas, Clayton (315) 686-2381; tifc@westel.com
- Doug Amos, Mallorytown, ON (613) 923-5257; damos@ripnet.com
- Pat Snyder, Alexandria Bay (315) 482-3750; abayfishing@gamil.com
- Dean Meckes, Clayton (315) 405-1706; deanmeckes@yahoo.com
- Bob Spivey, Mallarytown, ON (613) 923-5539; robertspivey@live.ca
- Larry Kirenhan, Alexandria Bay (315) 482-9368; bayguide@verizon.net
- James Dexter, Brockville, ON (613) 342-3102; Captain@chasenfish.com
- Tom Gillette, Clayton (315) 686-3017; fish@1000islandssportfishing.com
- Clayton Ferguson, Clayton (315) 686-3100; fergusonfishingcharters.com
- Dave Gascon, Alexandria Bay (315) 324-6800; fun2fish@cit-tele.com
- Randy Yager, Hammond (315) 324-3033; rryagerbasstrips.com
- Rice Rose, Alexandria Bay (315) 783-7155; captainric@verizon.net
- Eric Swensen, Cape Vincent (315) 654-2414; Ericjuli@sweenson@yahoo.com
- John Evan, Redwood (315) 785-9740; jevans@live.com
- Kevin White, Morrisburg ,ON (613) 543-6600; canadiancarp@sympatico.ca
- Walter Bonme, Clayton (315) 654-2673; lindavueadventures.com
- Rick Rose & John Evans, Alexandria Bay (315) 783-7155; ljevans@live.com
- Myrle Bauer, Clayton (315) 686-2122
- Matt Heath, Alexandria Bay (315) 408-6798; CaptainMatt@seawaycharters.com
- Rick Clarke, Clayton (315) 686-3041; sigman@1000islandsfishing.com
- Gene Snyder, Alexandria Bay (315) 686-5383
- Russ Finchout, Clayton (315) 686-1216
- Dan Roy, Lansdowne, ON (613) 659-3020; david@stlawrenceoutfitters.com

Forts

If you are a history buff, visit some of the forts for a day of family fun and education. You will get to learn about the history of the forts, visit museums, see re-enactments and much more.

FORT DE LA PRESENTATION
Route 68, Downtown Arterial Hwy.
Ogdensburg
(315) 394-1749
www.fort1749.org
Built in 1749, it is a mission fort named by the French Sulpician priest, Abbe Picquet. It was also sometimes known as Fort La Galette, built at the confluence of the Oswegatchie River and the St. Lawrence River. Enjoy the beautiful views, hike on Abbe Picquet Trail and visit the War of 1812 Peace Garden. Fort de La Presentation is an archaeological site.

FORT GEORGE VISITORS CENTER
Lake George Million Dollar Beach Bath House, Beach Road, Lake George.
(518) 623-1200 OR (518) 897-1200
www.visitadirondacks.com/attractions/heritage/fort-george-visitors-center
This new interpretive center features exhibits which recount the military and maritime history of Lake George from the earliest Native American presence through the end of the 18th century. On site is a historical marker and monument for the Radeau, Land Tortoise, which lies at the bottom of Lake George. The vessel is America's oldest intact warship and is on the National Register.

FORT TICONDEROGA
102 Fort Ti Road, Ticonderoga
(518) 585-2821
www.fortticonderoga.org
Fort Ticonderoga has much to offer visitors so plan to spend the day. Your family will have a fun-filled day starting with a visit to the museum. The museum staff will bring history to life with storytelling, historic trades, daily soldiers' life programs, weapons demonstrations, fife and drums, musket maintenance, shoe making, tailoring, and much more. The museum exhibits feature art, weapons and equipment from North America to Europe. While at Fort Ticonderoga, you will want to visit the 6-acre King's Garden and explore the centuries of garden history, fragrant heritage flowers and agricultural practices. Visit Mount Defiance for a view of Ticonderoga's epic military landscape. This is a tour offered daily May through October and enjoy lunch at the picnic pavilion at the top of the mountain. You can hike or drive up the mountain. Boat tours are also available. Some tours are included in ticket cost, so check out the website for further information. Fort Ticonderoga overlooks Lake Champlain and is about a 3-hour drive from Potsdam. For driving directions from other locations, visit the website. It is well worth the trip!

FORT WILLIAM HENRY
48 Canada Street, Lake George
(518) 668-5471
www.fwhmuseum.com
A British fort at the southern end of Lake George, New York. It is the site of notorious atrocities committed by the Huron tribes against the surrendered British and provincial troops following a successful French siege in 1757. Tour the museum buildings and view the many exhibits and artifacts related to the native American people that inhabited the area. Located inside the fort is the Sutler Shoppe offering a great selection of Fort William Henry and Lake George souvenirs. Tours are offered to school groups and there is an admission fee. They also have Ghost tours for those interested.

Golfing

If you love to be outdoors and enjoy golf, visit some of the many golf courses we have to offer. They range from par threes to the meticulous groomed and challenging courses. There is something for every level from beginner to expert golfers. Make it a family outing and bring your children. Many courses offer golf lessons for children.

CEDAR VIEW GOLF CLUB
462 NY 37C, Massena
(315) 705-4566
www.cedarviewgc.com
The 18-hole course features 6,027 yards of golf from the longest tees for a par 72. The course rating is 68.8 and has a slope rating of 119 on Rye grass. Cart rental and lounge available.

CLIFTON FINE MUNICIPAL GOLF COURSE
4173 Main Street, State Highway 3, Star Lake, (315) 848-357
www.cliftonfineadk.com
This course offers 9 holes, 2,799 yards, par 36, driving range, pro shop, cart rental, food.

DEERFIELD GOLF & COUNTRY CLUB
100 Craig Hill Drive, Brockport
(585) 392-8080
www.deerfieldcc.com
The 18-hole course was built on more than 350 acres with stunning scenery and challenging golf. With 5 sets of tees, the course will challenge and delight all players. The driving range, putting green, chipping green, practice bunker allows for a fun experience.

EMERALD GREENS GOLF COURSE
1485 US Highway 11, Gouverneur
(315) 287-4197
www.emeraldgreensgolf.com
The 9-hole course opened in 1970 and features 2,965 yards of golf from the longest tees for a par 35. The rating is 35.3 and it has a slope rating of 113 on Rye grass. Cart rental and lounge available.

FOX HILL GOLF & COUNTRY CLUB
216 Bailey Road, Massena
(315) 764-8633
www.foxhillgolfonline.com
This course offers 9 holes, 1,725 yards, par 31, pro shop, cart rental and food.

GOUVERNEUR COUNTRY CLUB
90 Country Club Road, off Rt. 58, Gouverneur
(315) 287-2130
www.gouverneurcountryclub.com
The 9-hole course 18 tees feature 6,379- yard layout with a rating of 70.1 and slope of 122. Cart rental and food available.

HIGHLAND GREENS GOLF COURSE
1055 State Route. 11b, Brushton
(518)-529-0563
www.highlandgreensgolf.com
The course offers 18 holes, club house (dining room and bar), an indoor Simulator Facility that offers real-world enhancements golfers experience on location. New imagery, championship tee boxes, panning views and varied pin placement are integrated. Simulator tee times by appointment only.

LANG BROOK MEADOW
95 Hamel Road off State Route 12, Brier
(315) 375-6372
www.langbrookmeadows.com
Built in 2002, this 18-hole, 5,766, par 71 course features challenging dog legs, ponds, and breathtaking views. Clubhouse, cart rental, lounge, and food.

MADRID GOLF COURSE
662 County Route 14, Madrid
(315) 322-0502
The course opened in 1997 and offers a 9-hole par-3 course, public golf course 27-par. Putting green and carts available.

MALONE GOLF CLUB
79 Golf Course Road, Malone
(518) 483-2926 or (518) 483-3633
www.malonegolfclub.com
This course offers 36 championship golf holes that is divided into two great golf courses. The East course is a par 72, with features that include roller coaster short par five and pure-links style bunkering. For a more challenging game, the West course is a par 71 with a diverse layout with major water hazards, sand bunkers and strong wind effect. Pro shop, restaurant, carts. Bring your family for a great outdoor activity.

MASSENA GOLF & COUNTRY CLUB
829 Route 131, Massena
(315) 769-2293
www.massenagolf.com
The 18-hole course's 6,670-yard design is a challenging par 71 course. The layout offers a view of the St Lawrence River from 14 of the 18 holes. Cart rental, food, showers available.

MEADOWBROOK GOLF COURSE
9757 US-11, Winthrop
(315) 389-4562
www.meadowbrookgolfny.com
This 9-hole course features 3,195 yards of golf from the longest tees for a par 36. Cart rental, snack bar.

PARTRIDGE RUN GOLF & COUNTRY CLUB
70 Sullivan Drive, Canton
(315) 386-4444
www.partridgerungolf.com
The course offers 18 holes, 6,569 yards, par 72, cart rental, pro shop, and food. They provide four tee options, great for beginners and seasoned pros. Yardages range from 5,200 to 6,700 yards. Also included is a putting green and twenty-station driving range. Children's lessons are available, and they also offer a junior golf academy.

POTSDAM TOWN & COUNTRY CLUB
6194 State Highway 56, Potsdam
(315) 265-2141
www.potsdamgolf.com
This course offers 18 holes, 6,508 yards, par 72, cart rental, full-length practice range, pro shop, lounge, food and showers. Featuring fast and true bent grass greens. They offer children's golf lessons every Wednesday.

RAYMONDVILLE GOLF & COUNTRY CLUB
Route 56, Raymondville
(315) 769-2759
Built in 1945, this 9-hole, 3,009-yard, par 36 course has much to offer.

ST. LAWRENCE STATE PARK GOLF COURSE
4955 NY-37, Ogdensburg
(315) 393-2286
The course is a 9-hole course that can be played twice from different tees for an 18-hole round. The course which sits within a 316-acre state park was designed to incorporate the view of the St. Lawrence River shipping channel and the Canadian shore. Visit the clubhouse and enjoy the food. Cart rental available.

ST. LAWRENCE UNIVERSITY GOLF COURSE
Route 11, 100 E. Main Street, Canton
(315) 386-4600
This course offers terrific views and challenging play for all golfers. The fairways and greens are well-groomed offering 18 holes, 6,800 yards, par 72, practice range, cart rental, lounge, shower, pro shop, and food.

TUPPER LAKE GOLF CLUB
141 Country Club Road, Tupper Lake
(518) 359-3701 www.tupperlakegolf.com
A scenic mountain course established in 1932. It has 18 holes, 6,250 yards, par 71, pro shop, practice range, and restaurant.

TWIN BROOKS GOLF COURSE
91 Franklin Road, Waddington
(315) 388-4031.
www.facebook.com/tbgolfcourse
The 18-hole course opened in 1963. It features 6,800 yards of golf from the longest tees for a par 71. The course rating is 70.0 and it has a slope rating of 113.

Guide Services

CRANBERRY LAKE GUIDE SERVICE
PO Box 571, Cranberry Lake 12927-0571
(315) 848-7346
www.northcountryguide.com

GRASSE RIVER ADVENTURES
An Adirondack guide service offering fully-guided, semi-guided and drop camp deer hunts, guided turkey hunts, guided fishing trips, guided camping trips, guided hikes and guided canoeing trips, offered from early spring through early winter, in the St. Lawrence Valley and northern Adirondack region of New York. Located at 436 County Route 47 Norwood,
www.grasseriveradventures.com
(315) 854-0422

PACKBASKET ADVENTURES, located on the banks of the Oswegatchie River on the edge of the Five Ponds Wilderness Area at 12 South Shore Road Extension in Wanakena. Open year-round by reservation to adults and children 12 years and older. Guide service available for paddling, hiking, biking, fishing, hunting and more. (315) 848-3488.
www.packbasketadventures.com

ST. REGIS CANOE OUTFITTERS, lightweight canoe and kayak rentals, shuttles and quality camping gear rentals, maps and guidebooks, guided trips. 73 Dorsey Street in Saranac Lake
www.canoeoutfitters.com
(518) 891-1838

Hayrides, Sleigh Rides, and Dog Sled Rides

CALL OF THE WILD SLED DOG TOURS is owned and operated by Carolyn and Spencer Thew. Spencer is an Iditarod veteran with 30 years of experience. Call of the Wild Sled Dog Tours South Colton, offers an Alaskan experience through year-round activities including sled dog rides (one-day or multi-day excursions) in the spring, fall and winter and kennel tours, presentations, parties and meet the dogs, plus hiking, nature tours and fishing in the summer. (315) 262-2145
www.callofthewildsleddingtours.com

CANTON CARRIAGE
385 Schoolhouse Road, Canton
(315) 854-4054
www.cantoncarriage.com

GORDON FAMILY FARM AND SAWMILL, 140 Kit Clark Road, Brushton, A sleigh for large groups is available, as well as a quaint old-fashioned sleigh for couples. (518) 529-7246
www.gordonfamilyfarmandsawmill.com

LAKE PLACID SLEIGH RIDES, 651 State Route 186, Saranac Lake (518) 949-8639.
www.nysleighrides.com

ST. LAWRENCE VALLEY DRAFT HORSE ASSOCIATION
www.stlawrencevalleydrafthorseclub.com

Hiking

The North Country is a hiker's paradise and a beginning hiker's dream. For decades now, dedicated outdoor enthusiasts have been sharing their knowledge and carefully mapping routes. Trails are maintained and improved through the volunteer efforts of not-for-profit organizations and government programs. From the valleys to the mountains, hiking trails of varying length and difficulty are well documented from a variety of resources.

In particular, The Adirondack Mountain Club has published and updated numerous guides over the years. Their books are available at local bookstores, online, and at their website: **www.adk.org** where members can buy at a discount.

With three pristine lakes to discover, and the Hoover of beaver dams, the Wolf Lake State Forest trails in Edwards are well worth your time. www.Stlsctrails.com

RESOURCES:

ST. LAWRENCE COUNTY:
www.stlsctrails.com
60 trails with descriptions, links to trail map, directions, and an interactive map

FRANKLIN COUNTY:
www.visitmalone.com – drop down bar: recreation/hiking
26 hikes, from downtown river walks to mountain treks, in and around Malone

Saddling St. Lawrence and Jefferson counties is The Grand Lake Reserve, offering a number of trails with overlooks to Butterfield Lake, Lake of the Woods and Grass Lake. www.Indian-RiverLakes.org

JEFFERSON COUNTY:
www.co.jefferson.ny.us/medical/Healthcare/trail-map-pdf.
Descriptions and directions for eight diversified trails from Alexandria Bay to Wellesley Island.

GREATER ADIRONDACK/ NORTH COUNTRY:
Kids on the Trail written by Potsdam residents Rose Rivizzi and David Trithart, is the bible for taking children on hikes in the Adirondacks. Second edition published in 2020.

www.ncpr.org/postcardmap – interactive audio postcard atlas – trek along with North Country Public Radio reporters and friends on their outdoor explorations and decide if this hike is for you.

www.ncpr.org/postcards – conventional chronological audio postcards

www.natureupnorth.org - "find a trail" - can filter for "difficulty" and "dogs allowed" comprehensive descriptions with links to trail maps

Offering a barrier-free Adirondack experience, John Dillon Park was designed under guidelines set by the Americans with Disabilities Act. Here, deep in the wilderness, are lean-tos, fishing docks and gentle trails built to accommodate wheelchairs. Overlooking Grampus Lake and Handsome Pond, the entrance is 20 miles south of Tupper Lake on Route 30. The park is free, open to all, and managed by Paul Smith's College.

Hockey

Clarkson University (Potsdam) and St. Lawrence University (Canton): Being only 10 miles apart, these two Universities host some of the most elite hockey teams each year for both men and women. All four teams attract North America and Europe's finest professional prospects. Over the years, the two schools have sent numerous players into the professional and Olympic ranks, including future Hall of Famer Dave Taylor (Clarkson '77) and Craig Conroy (Clarkson '94). Former Clarkson and St Lawrence men's players are on National Hockey League rosters. Alumni from the two Universities' men's teams have served as NHL players, coaches and General Managers. Clarkson women have won three National Championships in the last 6 years, including two Patty Kazmaier winners (Women's National Player of the Year). Tickets go fast during the height of the season, so be sure to reserve seats in advance by calling Appleton Arena at (315) 229-5423 or the Cheel Center at (315) 268-6622. Both arenas also offer general admission and standing room tickets at the box office on the night of the game. Be prepared to come early and stay late when these two long-time rivals square off against one another!

SUNY Potsdam and SUNY Canton also have Division III hockey for men and women which provides additional sporting events for all. SUNY Potsdam holds their athletic events at Maxcy Hall (315) 267-2000) 44 Pierrepont Avenue, Potsdam. SUNY Canton's men's and women's hockey is held at Roos House (315) 386-7051, 34 Cornell Drive, Canton.

CLARKSON UNIVERSITY MEN'S HOCKEY (GOLDEN KNIGHTS)
Cheel Arena, Cheel Main Street,
US Highway 11, Potsdam
(315) 268-6622
www.clarksonathletics.com

CLARKSON UNIVERSITY WOMEN'S HOCKEY (GOLDEN KNIGHTS)
Cheel Arena, Cheel Main Street,
US Highway 11, Potsdam
(315) 268-6622
www.clarksonathletics.com

SUNY POTSDAM MEN'S HOCKEY (BEARS)
44 Pierrepont Avenue,
Maxcy Hall, Potsdam
(315) 267-2000
www.potsdambears.com

SUNY POTSDAM WOMEN'S HOCKEY (BEARS)
44 Pierrepont Avenue,
Maxcy Hall, Potsdam
(315) 267-2000
www.potsdambears.com

ST. LAWRENCE UNIVERSITY MEN'S HOCKEY (SAINTS)
Augsbury Center, 23 Romoda Drive,
Canton
(315) 229-5423

ST. LAWRENCE UNIVERSITY WOMEN'S HOCKEY (SAINTS)
Augsbury Center, 23 Romoda Drive,
Canton
(315) 229-5423

SUNY CANTON MEN'S HOCKEY (ROOS)
SUNY Canton's Convocation,
Athletic and Recreation Center
Roos House, 34 Cornell Drive, Canton
(315) 386-7051
www.rooathletics.com

SUNY CANTON WOMEN'S HOCKEY (ROOS)
SUNY Canton's Convocation,
Athletic and Recreation Center
Roos House, 34 Cornell Drive, Canton
(315) 386-7051
www.rooathletics.com

Horseback Riding

A & J RIDING STABLE
342 County Route1, Hammond
(315) 324-6042

ADIRONDACK STABLE AND EQUESTRIAN CENTER LLC
87 Atwood Road, West Chazy
(518) 493-3211
www.adirondackstable.net
A fun place to learn how to ride and enjoy an equestrian experience. Along with stabling, they offer riding lessons for kids of all ages, birthday parties, and therapeutic riding.

ARTESIAN WELL STABLES
17540 Spencer Road, Watertown
(315) 782-6221

COLD RIVER TRAIL RIDES
3 Coreys Road, Tupper Lake
(518) 359-7559

COPPER TOP STABLES
4280 Branche Road, Cape Vincent
(315) 771-1644
www.coppertopstables.com
A full service boarding facility with an indoor arena, large turn-out pastures with lessons available upon appointment.

FAITH RIDING CENTER
21671 Red Road, Watertown
(315) 877-5212
A horseback riding facility where individuals of all abilities can come learn to ride and learn about all aspects of horsemanship.

GREYSTONE STABLES
26134 NY 12, Watertown
(315) 775-3005
Provides authentic, flexible care options for your horse.

HONEYDEW ACRES, LLC
169 Post Road, Canton
(315) 379-1035
www.honeydewacres.org
A family-owned equestrian facility that offers lessons, boarding and training.

NATURAL HORSE LOVER FARM
2130 NY Route 11-C, North Lawrence
(315) 389-5817
www.naturalhorseloverfarm.com
Offers coaching, riding lessons, confidence building, husbandry and more with indoor and outdoor facilities.

PONYLOVERZ CAMP AT SPENCER VALLEY FARM
28925 Rogers Road, Redwood

REIN TREE STABLES
325 Old Route 11, Canton
www.reintreestable.com
A full service boarding and training facility for horse and rider, specializing in hunter/jumper riding

SAND HILL STABLES
94 Trimm Road, St Regis Falls
(518) 856-0223
Boarding, training, lessons and leasing, in or outside.

ST. LAWRENCE UNIVERSITY STABLES Elsa Gunnison Appleton Riding Hall, Canton
(315) 229-5011

TWISTED TREE STABLES
15530 County Rod 155, Watertown
(315) 523-1096
www.twistedtreestables.com
A full service boarding and instruction barn

WILLOW HILL FARM
75 Cassidy Road, Keeseville
(518) 834-9746
www.willowhillfarm.com
Year-round programs include riding lessons, breeding, boarding, training and sales.

Ice Fishing

The Adirondacks has an abundance of water bodies and a reputation for long cold winters which makes it a natural fit for ice fishing. In addition, many of the lakes are not only scenic but they contain large trout and northern pike, along with abundant populations of yellow perch. Ice fishing generally starts in December after a few inches form on ponds and lakes, but the early season ice can be hard to predict because of thaws and changing weather patterns. You can learn more about ice fishing on the Department of Environmental Conservation website **www.dec.ny.gov**

ICE FISHING DERBIES AND TOURNAMENTS ARE HELD THROUGHOUT THE NORTH COUNTRY. Contact the county's chamber of commerce for information on what is scheduled and where it is held.

WONDERING WHERE TO DRILL THAT HOLE?

LAKE COLBY - Located near Saranac Lake, Lake Colby is a hot spot for fishermen in the winter. Usually a few anglers head out on the ice as soon as a few inches form in December. The lake is stocked with landlocked salmon, brown trout and rainbow trout, which are all popular targets in the winter months.

TUPPER LAKE - Located in Franklin County, Tupper Lake is one of the state's "hot spots" for large northern pike. The lake also contains large walleye and lake trout so anglers shouldn't have any problems finding big fish to target. One of the best times to head to the area is February when the local Rod and Gun clubs host the very popular Northern Challenge Ice Fishing Derby on Simond Pond, which is connected to Tupper Lake.

CRANBERRY LAKE - Located in St. Lawrence County, Cranberry Lake was traditionally one of the best brook trout fisheries in the Adirondacks during the warmer months.
Somewhere along the way, northern pike were introduced to the waters, which hurt the trout fishing but made it a desirable place to fish through the ice. Like Tupper Lake, the northern pike can be quite large. There are also plenty of yellow perch to be caught in its waters.

LOWER CHATEAUGAY LAKE - This lake has yellow perch in abundance along with Pumpkinseed and northern pike.

JONES POND - The Lake fills up early and has some excellent fishing near shore. Find Northern pike who like to browse in the deep weed beds.

OSGOOD POND - This pond is 500 acres of hungry pike and is known for "toothy action" and pike as big as 30 inches. The guides say "use big bait" and maybe use some of the smaller perch.

MEACHAM LAKE - This Lake is home to the "Big Bruiser" northern pike and good sized splake.

MOUNTAIN VIEW LAKE - Minutes from Malone, yet in a gorgeous wilderness, Mountain View Lake is one of the two great fishing lakes. A great place for ice fishing for pike.

ST. LAWRENCE RIVER - while most bays are productive, the popular areas include: Cape Vincent, Clayton, Wellesley Island (i.e. Eel Bay, Lake of the Isles), Alexandria Bay, Chippewa Bay, Ogdensburg, Wheathouse Bay and Cole's Creek. A tip up, a large minnow is an effective means of catching northern pike.

Ice Skating

St. Lawrence County has many lakes, ponds and rivers that freeze solid enough to skate on. However, it's better to play it safe in one of the many community rinks that are available. Community rinks may be found in the following towns: Canton, Clifton-Fine, Gouverneur, Louisville, Massena, Norwood, Potsdam, Brasher/Winthrop, and Waddington. Most town arenas make artificial ice from late fall to spring. In addition to skating, arenas offer the convenience of warming areas, concessions, and rest rooms.

Here is a partial list of ice arenas in the area. Many of these rinks host hockey tournaments and figure skating shows, so check ahead for schedules. Also, many of these rinks offer open skating hours as well as rental time in many cases:

CANTON
APPLETON ARENA, ST. LAWRENCE UNIVERSITY, Miner and Leigh streets, Canton. (315) 229-7260.

CANTON RECREATIONAL PAVILION, Outer Lincoln St. Canton, (315) 386-3992.

ROOS HOUSE ICE ARENA, SUNY Canton, 34 Cornell Drive, Canton, (315) 386-7051.

MASSENA
MASSENA ARENA, 180 Harte Haven Plaza, NYS Highway 37, Massena, municipal arena, (315) 769-3161.

SWAMPER DOME, LOUISVILLE COMMUNITY CENTER, County Routes 36 and 39, Louisville, (315) 769-8206.

TRI-TOWN ARENA, 746 NYS Highway 11C, Brasher Falls, (315) 389-4576.

OGDENSBURG
LOCKWOOD CIVIC CENTER, 141 West River Street, Ogdensburg, (315) 393-1980.

NEWELL MEMORIAL DOME AT OGDENSBURG FREE ACADEMY, 1100 State Street, Ogdensburg, (315) 393-5320.

POTSDAM
CHEEL ARENA, Clarkson University off NYS Highway 11 and Clarkson Avenue, Potsdam, (315) 268-7750.

PINE STREET ARENA, 43 Pine Street, Potsdam, village/town municipal rink, (315) 265-4030

MAXCY HALL ARENA, SUNY Potsdam, off Pierrepont Avenue, (315) 267-2000.

DOMINIC ZAPPIA COMMUNITY CENTER, 9 Clinton Street, Norfolk, (315) 384-3200.

STAR LAKE CLIFTON-FINE ARENA, 4173B State Highway 3, Star Lake, (315) 848-2578.

WADDINGTON DONALD MARTIN CIVIC CENTER, Pine Street, Waddington, (315) 388-4601.

Islands

Over 1,800 islands (1,864 to be exact) make up the 1000 Islands Region. To become an official part of the count, an island must meet two criteria: it must be above water 365 days a year and it must support two living trees. Ferries or bridges provide access to Wellesley, Hill, Wolfe and Howe Islands. The islands are unique, offering a wonderful recreation experience that spans two nations. Each island has its own individuality with features such as stately granite cliffs, soft sandy bays, tall dark pines and vibrant maple trees - it's a sightseer's paradise. Many islands are privately owned but ample public access can be found at island parks and villages throughout the region. French explorers named the region. Vacationers discovered the islands in the 1870s, when wealthy people began to build summer homes while other travelers came to stay in large hotels. For more than a century the area has been a mecca for summer visitors. In the more distant past the islands were stepping-stones between New York State and the Province of Ontario - in times of trouble between Canada and the United States, a place of refuge and a setting for disreputable deeds.

HILL ISLAND
716 Highway 137, Lansdowne, ON
1000 Islands Skydeck, Hill Island
(Lansdowne, Ontario)
(613) 659-2335
www.visit1000islands.com
A spectacular view of the 1000 Islands. The elevator takes 40 seconds to reach the first of three observation decks at 400 feet/130 meters above the St. Lawrence River. Tour guide, gift shops and food service.

ST. LAWRENCE ISLANDS NATIONAL PARK
County Road 5, R.R. #3,
Mallorytown, Ontario
(613) 923-5261, 800-839-8221
www.visit1000islands.com
Established in 1904, the Park currently comprises all or parts of 24 islands and about 90 islets scattered between the Main Duck Island and Brockville, Ontario, and a 100-acre mainland base at Mallorytown Landing. Visit for camping, sea kayaking, canoeing, picnicking, swimming and other outdoor recreation. Year round (limited access in winter), fees vary based on activity.

BOLDT CASTLE. HEART ISLAND
Alexandria Bay, NY
In Season: (315) 482-2501, Off Season: (315) 482-9724
www.boldtcastle.com
Take a romantic tour of Boldt Castle and be taken back in history. Boldt Castle is a six-story replica of a Rhineland Castle and belonged to George Boldt, the owner of the Waldorf Astoria. The Castle was a gift for his wife but was abandoned at her death just months away from completion. A tragic love story you don't want to miss!

DARK ISLAND
Chippewa Bay, Town of Hammond
(877) 327-5475
www.singercastle.com

Visitors will experience the mystery and unique history of the "hunting lodge" of Commodore Frederick Gilbert Bourne. Tour guides will take you on a 45-minute tour and narrative of the original castle. You will see four floors of artifacts, furnishings and secret passages. The massive medieval entranceway with Knights of Armor standing guard beside the marble fireplace is a sight you don't want to miss. The Drawing Room's four walls have elk, caribou, deer and moose mounted on them. Walk up the marble stairway where large Gothic windows have a breathtaking view of the St. Lawrence River. Make sure to wear comfortable shoes and bring your camera! No strollers are allowed in the Castle.

For a romantic visit on a special occasion, treat yourself to a full adventure of Singer Castle. Take the opportunity and stay the night in the Royal Suite, complete with private modern bath, luxury furnishings and more. In the evening you will marvel at the breathtaking views of the Canadian sunset and in the morning, the American sunrise. You will feel like the King of the Castle! Included in the package is an extended private tour, catered dinner, continental breakfast and more. A shuttle service to and from the Island is available. Schermerhorn Harbor Shuttle, Hammond. (315) 324-5966 or visit the web at www.schermerhornharbor.com

LIST OF TOP ISLANDS IN ST. LAWRENCE COUNTY
www.anyplaceamerica.com/directory/ny/st-lawrence-county-36089/islands

LIST OF ISLANDS IN ST. LAWRENCE COUNTY
www.newyork.hometownlocator.com/features/physical,class,island,scfips,36089.cfm

LIST OF ISLANDS IN JEFFERSON COUNTY
www.newyork.hometownlocator.com/features/physical,class,island,scfips,36045.cfm

LIST OF TOP ISLANDS IN FRANKLIN COUNTY
www.anyplaceamerica.com/directory/ny/franklin-county-36033/islands

Libraries

If you are looking for a book to read, a computer to use, a movie to watch, a workshop to participate in, or a story hour to listen to, check out one of the area libraries. The North Country Library system has 65 different public library locations offering a rich variety of resources, classes, and community events, as well as a wealth of online materials you can explore. Many of these libraries host a local Battle of the Books competition for students in grades 4-6, ESL and literacy classes, family game or movie nights, and even potluck dinners. Some offer unique collections to borrow (Canton has a tool library!) or even a seed library to select from in the spring/summer months. Check individual websites for details or phone for story-time hours, vacation programs, open hours, and classes.

NORTH COUNTRY LIBRARY SYSTEM
www.ncls.org

MACSHERRY LIBRARY
112 Walton Street, Alexandria Bay
(315) 482-2241
www.macsherrylibrary.org

CROSBY PUBLIC LIBRARY
59 Main Street, Antwerp
(315) 659-8564 www.crosbylibrary.org

SALLY PLOOF HUNTER MEMORIAL LIBRARY 101 Public Works Drive, Black River (315) 773-5163
www.sallyploofhunterlibrary.org

BROWNVILLE GLEN PARK LIBRARY
216 Brown Boulevard, Brownville
(315) 788-7889
www.brownvillelibrary.org

CANTON FREE LIBRARY
8 Park Street, Canton (315) 386-3712
Also branches in Morley and Rensselaer Falls
www.cantonfreelibrary.org

CARTHAGE FREE LIBRARY
412 Budd Street, Carthage
(315) 493-2620
www.carthagefreelibrary.org

HAWN MEMORIAL LIBRARY
220 John Street, Clayton (315) 686-3762
www.hawnmemoriallibrary.org

HEPBURN LIBRARY
84 Main Street, Colton (315) 262-2310
www.coltonhepburnlibrary.org

CLIFTON COMMUNITY LIBRARY
7171 State Highway 3, Cranberry Lake
(315) 848-3256
www.cliftoncomlib.org

DEPAUVILLE FREE LIBRARY
32333 County Route 179, Depauville
(315) 686-3299
www.Depauvillefreelibrary.org

EVANS MILLS PUBLIC LIBRARY
8706 Noble Street, Evans Mills
(315) 629-4483
www.evansmillspubliclibrary.org

GOUVERNEUR PUBLIC LIBRARY
60 Church Street, Gouverneur
(315) 287-0191
www.gouverneurlibrary.org

HAMMOND FREE LIBRARY
17 Main Street, Hammond
(315) 324-5139
www.hammondfreelibrary.org

HARRISVILLE FREE LIBRARY
8209 Main Street, Harrisville
(315) 543-2577
www.harrisvillefreelibrary.org

HEPBURN LIBRARY OF HERMON
105 Main Street, Hermon (315) 347-2285
www.hermonhepburnlibrary.org

HEUVELTON FREE LIBRARY
57 State Street, Heuvelton (315) 344-6550
www.heuveltonfreelibrary.org

HOPKINTON READING CENTER
7 Church Street, Hopkinton
(315) 328-4113
www.hopkintonnylibrary.org

ORLEANS PUBLIC LIBRARY
36263 State Route 180, Lafargeville
(315) 658-2271
www.lafargevillelibrary.org

LAKE PLACID PUBLIC LIBRARY
2471 Main Street, Lake Placid
(518) 523-3200
www.lakeplacidlibrary.org

HEPBURN LIBRARY OF LISBON
6899 County Route 10, Lisbon
(315) 393-0111
www.hepburnlibraryoflisbon.org

HEPBURN LIBRARY OF MADRID
11 Church Street, Madrid
(315) 322-5673
www.hepburnlibraryofmadrid.org

MASSENA PUBLIC LIBRARY
41 Glenn Street, Massena
(315) 769-9914
www.massenapubliclibrary.org

MORRISTOWN PUBLIC LIBRARY
200 Main Street, Morristown
(315) 375-8833
www.morristownpubliclibrary.org

HEPBURN LIBRARY OF NORFOLK
1 Hepburn Street, (315) 384-3052
www.hepburnlibraryofnorfolk.org

NORWOOD PUBLIC LIBRARY
1 Morton Street, (315) 353-6692
www.norwoodnylibrary.org

OGDENSBURG PUBLIC LIBRARY
312 Washington Street, Ogdensburg
(315) 393-4325
www.ogdensburgpubliclibrary.org

BODMAN MEMORIAL LIBRARY
8 Aldrich Street, Philadelphia
(315) 642-3323
www.bodmanmemoriallibrary.org

POTSDAM PUBLIC LIBRARY
2 Park Street, Potsdam (315) 265-7230
www.potsdamlibrary.org

RICHVILLE FREE LIBRARY
87 Main Street, Richville (315) 287-1481
www.richvillefreelibrary.org

RUSSELL PUBLIC LIBRARY
24 Pestle Street, Russell (315) 347-2115
www.russellpubliclibrary.org

SARANAC LAKE FREE LIBRARY
109 Main Street, Saranac Lake
(518) 891-4190 www.slfl.org

THERESA FREE LIBRARY
301 Main Street, Theresa (315) 628-5972
www.theresafreelibrary.org

HEPBURN LIBRARY OF WADDINGTON
30 Main Street, Waddington
(315) 388-4454
www.waddingtonlibrary.org

FLOWER MEMORIAL LIBRARY
229 Washington Street, Watertown
(315) 785-7705
www.flowermemoriallibrary.org

The area college and university libraries welcome the North Country community to use their spaces and resources as well. You can sign up for a community member card to check out books, and you can get research help from the librarians. Please note, access to these libraries' online resources is only possible on site, not remotely. It helps to phone ahead of your visit.

CLARKSON UNIVERSITY
www.clarkson.edu Main Library, main Clarkson campus, 8 Clarkson Avenue, Potsdam (315) 268-2292
Health Sciences Library, downtown campus, 59 Main Street, Potsdam (315) 268-4462

ST. LAWRENCE UNIVERSITY
www.stlawu.edu 23 Romoda Drive, Canton, Owen D. Young Library, Main campus library (315) 229-5451
Launders Science Library (315) 229-5400

SUNY POTSDAM
www.library.potsdam.edu
44 Pierrepont Avenue, Potsdam
Crumb Memorial Library (315) 267-2485
Crane Music Library (315) 267-2451

SUNY CANTON
www.canton.edu/library
34 Cornell Drive, Canton
Southworth Library Learning Commons
(315) 386-7011

Lighthouses

Cape Vincent and Golden Crescent offer some of the most breathtaking scenery in the region. Classic maritime villages nestled in sheltered bays, provide points of departure for fresh-water recreation of all kinds. Cape Vincent has a strong French heritage. After Bonaparte's brother, Joseph, established residence here in the early 1800s, Napoleon Bonaparte was also to have settled there, seeking refuge. The village celebrates its history with the colorful French Festival held around Bastille Day on the second Saturday in July.

GALLOO ISLAND LIGHTHOUSE
Town of Hounsfield, Jefferson County
Galloo Island light is a historic lighthouse that is privately owned. It is found six miles off the mainland of Galloo Island on the South Western side of the island. The lighthouse is a fixed white light producing a beam that is visible up to 15 miles. It also consists of a steam whistle that it sounds when the weather turns foggy. The whistle blows for 10 seconds and then it is silent for 30 seconds. The island does not have a harbor and only accessible using smaller boats. Today it stands tall and abandoned.

TIBBETTS POINT LIGHTHOUSE
33435 County Route 6, Cape Vincent
(315) 654-2700
www.capevincent.org
Located less than three miles west of Cape Vincent where the great Lake Ontario empties into the St. Lawrence River, this historic lighthouse shares Tibbetts Point with an American Youth Hostel that is open from May to October. There is also a visitor's center, museum and gift shop on the grounds.

ROCK ISLAND LIGHTHOUSE
St. Lawrence River, Jefferson County
www.claytonislandtours.com
Rock Island Lighthouse is on a four-acre State Park on Rock Island. Climb up the lighthouse tower to look over the St. Lawrence River and view the magnificent views of the surrounding area and take some memorable photos. You can access the island by private or chartered boat. For an adventure, take the Night Heron, a glass-bottomed boat and see the incredible underwater life of native fish and other natural wonders. Public boat tours are available in Clayton. Grass Point State Park is the nearest public launch site that is approximately five minutes away from the island. They also have a museum you can enjoy. There is a fee for access.

CAPE VINCENT BREAKWATER LIGHTHOUSE
Route 12E, Cape Vincent
www.lighthousefriends.com
The one surviving wooden tower stands beside Route 12E on the southern outskirts of Cape Vincent, now welcoming travelers arriving by land.

SACKETS HARBOR LIGHTHOUSE
Horse Island, Sackets Harbor, Jefferson County
www.lighthousefriends.com
The 24-acre island was acquired by the Civil War Trust for preservation. This site was used as a staging area during the War of 1812, before the Battle of Sacket's Harbor. For history buffs this is a place to visit.

WEBSITE FOR LIGHTHOUSES IN JEFFERSON COUNTY
www.topozone.com/new-york/jefferson-ny/lighthouse

WEBSITE FOR LIGHTHOUSES IN NEW YORK STATE
www.lighthousefriends.com

MAP OF LIGHTHOUSES IN NEW YORK STATE
www.google.com/maps/d/viewer?mid=-1oGyMIObWsD3j8MeRlWUxCZUWB-JA&ll=42.69058216963644%2C-75.72594500000002&z=7

Maple Syrup Tours

MAPLE LEAF FARM
120 Coon Road, Canton
(315) 386-2460
(by appointment only).
Oil-fire state of the art maple syrup operation with 2,000 pipeline taps in season.

SUNDAY ROCK MAPLE
PO Box 432, Route 56, South Colton
(315) 262-2467
(by appointment only).
This maple syrup operation demonstrates state of the art maple syrup production while maintaining the old-time sugar bush. 2,300 taps using buckets and tubing.

FARMHOUSE MAPLE
14685 Bay Breeze Way, Dexter
(315) 486-5981
www.farmhousemaple.com
The farm has a 50-acre maple forest that has the remnants of the old farm buildings and sugar shack. They produce many maple products for your enjoyment. Take home some of their maple BBQ sauce, maple dips, maple toffee popcorn, and more. If you have a special person you want that unusual gift for, you can create baskets of maple products that they will ship.

FRIEND'S MAPLE PRODUCTS
402 Spencer Road, Burke
(518) 483-5559
Enjoy a free wagon ride and see where the sap is collected during Maple Weekend. Your children will enjoy a visit to the sugarhouse and learn about the process of making maple syrup. If you are interested in purchasing maple products, they have a variety of goodies including candies, coated nuts, cotton candy, maple cream and syrup.

LAKESIDE MAPLE SYRUP
298 Narrows Road, Chateaugay Lake
(518) 569-9951

> PURE MAPLE SYRUP IS A SOURCE OF NUTRITION AND ENERGY. IT'S A NATURAL SWEETENER USED IN MANY BAKED GOODS AND FOR MAKING DELICIOUS MAPLE CANDY!

www.facebook.com/LaClair-LakesideMaple. Tour the sugarhouse to see the 2' x 8' oil/fire evaporator with reverse osmosis technology and sample the maple syrup and maple cream. They offer Adirondack pure maple syrup and cream, local pure raw honey, creamed cinnamon honey, and 100% natural and organic Beeswax Lip Balm.

MASSEY RANCH
20605 Combs Road, Watertown
(315) 786-5939
www.masseysranch.com
With over 500 trees tapped, they produce syrup, maple candy, maple cream and maple cotton candy. The ranch has a 5-acre pumpkin patch, a selection of gourds and Indian corn. Try the wagon ride through the patch for a fun time with your family.

MOON VALLEY MAPLE
215 Johnson Road, Malone
(518) 483-3740
www.moonvalleymaple.com
Moon Valley Maple offers tours of the facility to schools, groups, and clubs. You will tour the sugar lines, do hands-on activities, sample products and enjoy lunch in their cafeteria. Stop by for free samples and tours of the sugarhouse on Maple Weekend.

RUDD'S FAMILY MAPLE SYRUP
16370 Balch Place, Mannsville
(315) 405-1479
www.facebook.com/RuddsFamilyMaple
Visit their warm sugar house to see the boiling process of the maple syrup and sample the maple products. They have maple cream, maple sugar cakes, maple candy, popcorn and more.

THE OREBED
503 Orebed Road, DeKalb Junction
(315) 347-3415
www.orebedmaplesugarshack.com
This family owned and operated sugar shack produces organic maple products, unique wedding favors and corporate gifts. Enjoy the maple syrup, maple cream, maple candy and they also make maple granulated sugar. If you are interested learning how maple syrup is collected, take the free guided tour and try your hand a tapping a tree. Call ahead for group tours.

WINTER HARVEST SUGAR SHACK
409 Wagner Road, North Bangor
(518) 353-8728
www.facebook.com/Winters-Harvest-Sugar-Shack
If you want to try something unique, stop by the sugarhouse for demonstrations and taste their maple jack BBQ sauce and bourbon barrel aged maple syrup.

WOODS MAPLE PRODUCTS
1470 County Route 23, Chateaugay
(518) 497-6387
www.woodsmaple.com
Enjoy the demonstrations and tour of the sugaring operations. Their store offers a full range of maple products including cream, jelly candies, syrup and granulated sugar.

Marinas

All of the marinas listed here, with the exception of Cranberry Lake in the Adirondack Mountains, are on the St. Lawrence River, which forms the border between New York State and Canada. If you are traveling "down river" on the St. Lawrence, you're actually traveling north, from the Thousand Islands region in Jefferson County, past the St Lawrence County communities of Hammond, Morristown, Ogdensburg, Waddington and Massena.

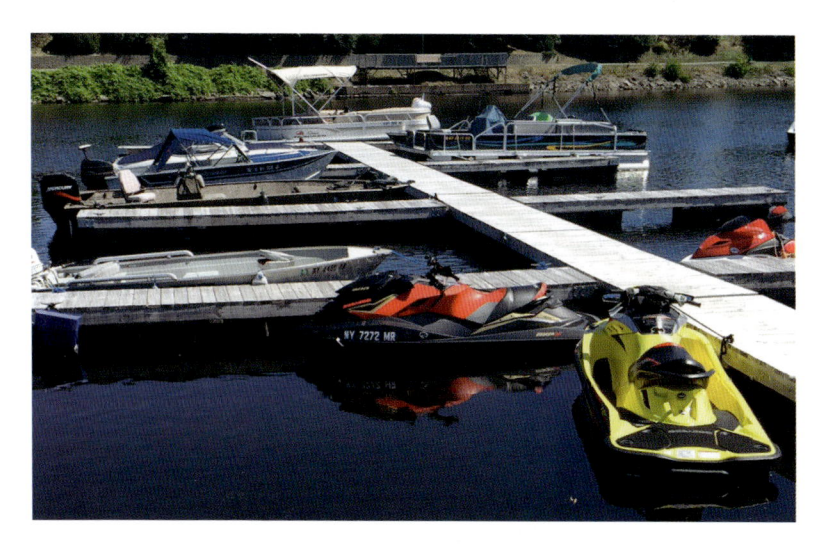

ALEXANDRIA BAY

BONNIE CASTLE YACHT BASIN
Holland Street, Alexandria Bay.
(315) 482-2526 or 1-800-955-4511
www.bonniecastle .com.

EDGEWOOD MARINA Edgewood Park Road, Alexandria Bay. (315) 482-9923 or 888 Edgewood (334-3966)
www.theedgewoodresort .com

WHEN YOU'RE OUT BOATING ON THE ST. LAWRENCE RIVER a great place to dock and have a bite to eat is Hosmer's Marina and Smuggler's Café at 54 East River Street in Ogdensburg. Located at the mouth of the Oswegatchie River, just off the St. Lawrence, Hosmer's offers you a place to dock, fill your boat with gas and stock up on supplies. You can also chat with the staff about the best places to fish and enjoy other water recreation in the area. Next-door is Smuggler's Café that offers a great menu, with everything from sandwiches to wraps to salads, wings, burgers and pizza that you can enjoy either inside or out on the patio. Check out their menu at **www.hosmersmarina.com**

LEDGES RESORT MOTEL & MARINA
71 Anthony Street, Alexandria Bay
(315) 482-9334 or 877-233-9334
www.ledgesresort.com

O'BRIENS BOAT RENTALS
51 Walton Street, Alexandria Bay
(315) 482-9548 or 800-633-9548

H. CHALK & SON
35 Main Street,
Fishers Landing
(315) 686-5622
www.hchalk.com

HORIZON MARINE
22 Sisson Street,
Alexandria Bay
(315) 482-9956
www.horizon-marine.com

HUTCHINSON'S BOAT WORKS
27 Holland Street,
Alexandria Bay
(315) 482-9931
www.hutchinsons-boatworks.com

INLET HARBOR CLUB PINE TREE POINT RESORT
Alexandria Bay
(315) 482-9911
or 888-PINE BAY
(746-3229) www.pinetreepointresort.com

R.C. CONGEL BOATS NORTH
45447 State Highway 12, Alexandria Bay
(315) 482-5109 www.rccongelboats.com

RIVEREDGE RESORT 17 Holland Street, Alexandria Bay (315) 482-9917 or 800 ENJOY US (365-6987)
www.riveredge.com

ROGERS MARINA
16 Bethune Street
Alexandria Bay. (315) 482-9461

SWAN BAY RESORT
43615 State Highway 12, Alexandria Bay, RV park cottage rentals and marina
(315) 482-SWAN

VAN'S MOTOR MARINA
20 Sisson Street, Alexandria Bay
(315) 482-2271

VILLAGE OF ALEXANDRIA BAY DOCKS
Upper James Street Dock, Alexandria Bay
(315) 482-9902

WELLESLEY ISLAND YACHT CLUB
Thousand Islands Country Club
(315) 482-9454 or
1-800-928-TICC (8422)
www.ticountryclub.com

CLAYTON

REMAR SHIPYARD & RENTALS
510 Theresa Street, Clayton
(315) 686-4170 (shipyard)
(315) 686-3579 (rentals) houseboats.
www.gordonsguide.com
www.remarrentalsinc.com

CRANBERRY LAKE

THE EMPORIUM State Route 3. (315) 848-2140. Offers bait, tackle, boat rentals, dockage.

HAMMOND

BLIND BAY MARINA 115 Blind Bay Road, Hammond, (315) 324-5350

CHAPMAN'S MARINA Black Lake Rd. (315) 324-5265. Sporting goods, boat supplies, bait and tackle.

SCHERMERHORN MARINA CENTER 71 Schermerhorn Landing Road (315) 324-5966. Full service marina. www.schermerhomlanding.com

SKIPPERS MARINA AT BLIND BAY 115 Blind Bay Road. (315) 324-5350. Slips, rentals, bait & tackle, groceries, boat supplies, pool, playground, showers.

MASSENA

BARNHART ISLAND MARINA Beach Road. (315) 764-0022. Dock, ramp, fuel, mooring, water & pump-out facility, boat slips, electric, marine supplies and launch.

MORRISTOWN

WRIGHT'S SPORTING GOODS & MARINA 511 Main Street (315) 375-8841. Docks, gas and ice, groceries, rest rooms, water, marine supplies, bait, marine sales and service.

OGDENSBURG

HOSMER'S MARINA 54 East River Street, Restaurant, snacks, ice, bait shop, assorted tackle, fishing poles and nets, boating supplies, gas, docking, rentals. (315) 393-3324 www.hosmersmarina.com

THE TACKLE BOX 54 River Street (315) 393-0831. Offers gas, docking, bait, marine services, rest rooms, tackle, marine supplies, ramp.

OGDENSBURG MUNICIPAL MARINA 100 Riverside Avenue, (315) 393-1980. Docking, pumpout, electric, water, rest rooms, showers.

RAMADA INN RIVER RESORTS MARINA (315) 393-2222. Docks, gas, electric, restaurant, rooms, rest rooms.

WADDINGTON

COLES CREEK MARINA 13135 State Highway 37, Massena-Waddington Road. (315) 388-4237. Dock rest rooms, ramp, boat lift, storage, marine supplies, fuel, water & pump-out facility, slips with electric.

WADDINGTON MARINA St. Lawrence Avenue. (315) 388-4433. Docks.

Miniature Golf

BLACK LAKE MINI GOLF
2626 CR 6, Hammond
(315) 375-8965
www.fishingny.com/funstuff
This 18-hole course is fun and challenging for everyone. They have a frequent golfer card that when you play 3 paid games, you get one game free. If you hit the ball in the clown's nose on the 18th hole, you win the cash jackpot. They also offer birthday parties, food, batting cages and water wars.

JUNGLE FUN MINI PUTT
(315) 250-7381
6100 St. Lawrence Centre, Massena
www.stlawrencecentre.com
Jungle Fun is a year-round nine-hole mini-putt center that is lit with a black light, making the course more challenging than those outdoors. Everything is painted with a fluorescent paint and each hole will have something different to do.

RIVER ADVENTURE GOLF
40168 NYS Route 12, Clayton
(315) 777-0225

www.rivergolfadventures.com
This water theme 18-hole mini golf course has much to offer for all ages. You can enjoy this state-of-the-art driving range, Bumper Boats, River Mining Gem Sluice, Pirates Treasure Dig, Arcade. They also host birthday parties. Your family will enjoy the whole day here!

SWINGTIME MINI GOLF
7065 US 11, Potsdam
(315) 212-9975
www.swingtimeminigolf.com
Opened in 2015, this unique mini golf course has much to offer. Also available for parties and/or live music is a Gazebo.

TIMEQUEST MINI GOLF
9987 NY 56, Massena
(315) 514-7253
www.facebook.com/timequestminigolf
A fun place to visit that offers two 18-hole mini-golf courses, a small petting zoo with goats, ducks, and chickens, large party room with 2 big screen TVs, and handicap accessible restrooms. Snacks and drinks are available.

Mountain Biking

St. Lawrence County boasts a good amount of mountain bike-specific trails. There is a trail system on Lenny Road in Colton that has everything from beginner flow trails to advanced technical terrain. There is also an area called Seven Springs in Wildwood in the High Flats State Forest (Colton/Parishville). Further away, in Palmerville, is Downerville State Forest which has a mix of 17 trails. Clarkson University in Potsdam has miles of winding mountain bike trails. Most are unmarked and not maintained, except for a few main jump lines. Other than the jump lines, everything is beginner. You'll find the area, known as the Clarkson Woods, near the water tower.

> www.STLCtrails.com has complete information, with trail maps, for eight different trails in St. Lawrence County. There is also an app called TrailForks that has maps of all the local MTB trails, designates where parking is, and the difficulty of every trail.

Movie Theaters

AMERICAN THEATRE (5 SHOWINGS/MATINEES)
98 Main Street, Canton
(315) 386-2981
www.jscinemas.com

ROXY THEATER (5 SHOWINGS/MATINEES)
20 Main Street, Potsdam
(315) 265-9630
www.jscinemas.com

MASSENA MOVIE PLEX (9 SHOWINGS/MATINEES)
Harte Haven Shopping Center, Massena
(315) 769-1268
www.jscinemas.com

STATE THEATER (2 SHOWINGS)
100 Park Street, Tupper Lake
(518) 359-3593
www.tupperlakemovies.com

REGAL SALMON RUN STADIUM (12 SHOWINGS/MATINEES)
Address: 21182 Salmon Run Mall Loop W, Watertown
(315) 782-2843
www.shopsalmonrunmall.com/tenants/regal-cinemas

> **TIPS:** FOR CURRENT MOVIE LISTINGS AND TIMES BE SURE TO VisiT the websites of individual theaters

Museums

ADIRONDACK LAKES CENTER FOR THE ARTS, Blue Mountain Lake, Route 28, (518) 352-7715, adirondackarts.org
Gallery Exhibits, Special Event

ADIRONDACK EXPERIENCE, THE MUSEUM ON BLUE MOUNTAIN LAKE, Route 30, Blue Mountain Lake, (518) 352-7311, **www.theadkx.org** Storytellers for life in the park, past and present. Twenty-three buildings and structures span across 121 acres. Daily programs. Artists in Residence. Open late May through mid October. Admission fee valid for two consecutive days. Indoor dining and picnic areas.

ADIRONDACK PARK VISITOR INTERPRETIVE CENTER, Route 30, Paul Smiths, (518) 327-6241, vic@paulsmiths.edu. Connecting outdoor recreation, experiential education, and the arts. Butterfly House, Exhibits Free. Open 9-5 daily; open weekends, November 30-April 1; open 7 days a week, holiday weeks.

ANTIQUE BOAT MUSEUM, 750 Mary Street, Clayton, (315) 686-4104 **www.abm.org** Admission includes free rowing and sailing (call ahead). Motor cruises offered for additional fee. Seasonal hours. Stroll the collection of antique boats, motors and engines. Museum campus and exhibit buildings are wheelchair accessible, with paved paths.

BETH JOSEPH SYNAGOGUE, 57 Lake Street, Tupper Lake, (315) 347-3580, **www.tupperlake.com** Built in 1905, the oldest synagogue in the Adirondacks, offers guided tours, Tuesday through Friday, 11am-3pm, in July and August. Home to an art gallery and museum of Jewish life in the Adirondacks.

CANTON TOWN AND VILLAGE COLLECTION, Canton Municipal Building, Main Street, Second Floor, (315) 386-1633. A mini-museum with town/village archives, photographs, maps/artifacts. By appointment.

COLTON MUSEUM AND HISTORICAL SOCIETY, 96 Main Street, (315) 262-2524, **www.nyheritage.org** Large collection of photographs and postcards covering a 150 year period.
Call for hours

GOUVERNEUR MUSEUM, 30 Church Street, (315) 287-0570, **www.gouverneurmuseum.com**. Open Wednesdays & Saturdays, 1:00pm-3:00pm, or by appointment. Three floors of artifacts and galleries.

HAMMOND HISTORICAL MUSEUM, 1A North Main Street, (315) 324-6628, **www.hammondmuseum.com**.
Call or check website for seasonal hours. Large collection of miniature buildings, crafted in the early 1900s. Celebrates Hammond's Scottish settlers with a Scottish Festival each summer.

HOPKINTON HISTORICAL GROUP AND MUSEUM, www.**townofhopkinton.com**, hopkintonhistoricalgroup@gmail.com for hours or appointment. Housed in the recently renovated Trask House in the center of the village, exhibits include an early home life, local military history, Sara's Store, and an early classroom.

THE LISBON MUSEUM DEPOT, (315) 393-4154 – call for hours
A collection of railroad related artifacts from days gone by, and also a vast display of historic items detailing Lisbon's history in a reclaimed and restored railroad depot from the Rutland Railroad era.

CELINE G. PHILIBERT MEMORIAL CULTURE CENTRE & MUSEUM (Massena Museum), 79 Main Street, Massena. Tuesday through Saturday, 10:00 a.m. to 4:00 p.m. Local history collection of photographs, Civil War artifacts, folk art, farm and ice cutting tools, period furnishings, antique toys and school items. The Massena Aluminum Historical Association's display illustrates the importance of aluminum to the community. Exhibits are mounted in the Culture Centre.

MORRISTOWN GATEWAY MUSEUM, 309 Main Street, www.morristowngatewaymuseum.org. Memorial Day – September 29. Saturday, 9am-1pm, Sunday 1pm-4pm, Wednesday, 9am-1pm. Provides a full summer of concerts, lectures, classes and displays. View memorabilia and photographs, a re-created blacksmith shop, ice house, an antique car collection and a Civil War military display. The Morristown area has many historic buildings and stone structures, including an 1825 stone windmill and 1824 stone school house.

NORFOLK HISTORICAL MUSEUM, 42-1/2 West Main Street, Norfolk. (315) 384-4575. **www.norfolknymuseum.com**. Tuesdays and Thursdays, 12pm-5pm, year round or by appointment.

North Country Children's Museum, *where kids play to learn & grown-ups learn to play*
10 Raymond St., Potsdam (315) 274-9380 **www.northcountrychildrensmuseum.org** $8.00 admission per person. Members and children under 12 months: Free. Wednesday through Sunday, 10:00am-5:00pm.
Hands-on, Minds-on STEAM education for families. Children of all ages play, imagine, discover and learn through interactive exhibits and programs. This is a space for kids to become scientists, engineers and artists. Run the store at Kid's Co-op & Bakery; use real materials and tools in the Construction Zone; learn about river waterways and hydropower at Adirondack Waterplay. Playspace provides a calm, creative space for younger children to explore sensory activities and develop motor skills. There are changing pop-up creative play tables daily as well as theme days, special activities, programs, events, and camps.

THE NORTHERN NEW YORK AGRICULTURAL HISTORICAL SOCIETY AGRICULTURAL MUSEUM, 30950 Route 180, LaFargeville. (315) 658-2353. www.stonemillsmuseum.org. 11am through 3pm and by appointment. A museum that tells the story of the development of agriculture in Northern New York, includes a sawmill, granary, school house, church and many display buildings.

SUSAN C. LYMAN HISTORICAL MUSEUM, (Norwood Museum) 39 Main Street, Norwood, (315) 353-2751. May-November, Tuesday and Thursday, 2:00 p.m. to 4:00 p.m. and by appointment. Browse through the local history displays in a historic home. View an exhibit dedicated to the Norwood Brass Firemen's Band.

OLD METHODIST MEETINGHOUSE MUSEUM, 696 East DeKalb Road, DeKalb Junction. (315) 347-1900. www.Dekalbnyhistorian.org. Wednesday, 11:00am-3:00pm, Thursdays, 4:00pm-7:00pm, and by appointment. Local history, virtual archives, searchable indexes, classroom toolkit and special events.

PARISHVILLE MUSEUM, East Main Street, (315) 265-7619, **www.parishvilleny.us**. Historical home contains history, artifacts, archives and an entire collection of hand-carved circus miniatures.

PIERREPONT MUSEUM, 868 State Highway 68, (315) 386-8311, May-August, Saturdays 10:00am – 2:00pm. Housed in an early 1800 district school house displays exhibits of a rural schoolhouse, farm tools of the pre-machine era, veterans exhibit, text books, kitchen artifacts, clothing, paintings and biographies of local artists.

POTSDAM PUBLIC MUSEUM, Civic Center, 2 Park Street, (315) 265-6910, **www.potsdampublicmuseum.org**. Local history museum and public archive containing cemetery records, military and census records, family files, Civil War, WWI and WWII, directories, maps, a collectibles and reference library. Offers assistance with research and genealogy. Hosts musical events and lectures throughout the year as well as rotating exhibits from the museum collections.

FREDERIC REMINGTON ART MUSEUM, 303 Washington Street, Ogdensburg, (315) 393-2425, **www.fredericremington.org** Adults - $9, Seniors and Students - $8, Military $5. Dedicated to collecting, exhibiting, preserving and interpreting the art and archives of Frederic Remington, it showcases paintings, bronze sculptures and personal items. The museum offers year-round educational programs for children, teens, adults and families. The museum is also home to The Learning Gardens. Seven gardens of flowers, vegetables, trees, bird houses, and water pond. Picnic tables and an "eye spy" game for children.

In a separate building, the Remington Art Museum has created Kid's Place, a children's museum, featuring dynamic interactive exhibits, opportunities for creative play, and art activities created expressly for children of different ages and learning abilities. A fully staffed kids' art studio is stocked with art materials and projects. Kid's Place is always free to children and their caregivers.

RICHVILLE HISTORICAL MUSEUM, Main Street, (315) 287-0562. Open by appointment.

ST. LAWRENCE-FDR POWER PROJECT'S HAWKINS POINT VISITORS CENTER, 800 Barnhardt Island Road, Massena. 800-262-6972
Open Memorial Day-Labor Day, daily, 9:30am-6pm. Labor Day-Columbus Day, daily 9am-4:30pm, Columbus Day-Memorial Day, Mon-Fri, 9am-4:30pm. Free. The Visitors Center at the power dam features state-of-the-art exhibits on energy, electricity and the area's history. From the viewing deck you can watch huge tankers and ships being lifted or lowered 42 feet in the lock chamber. Call ahead to determine when ships will be arriving at the locks: (315) 769-2422.

ST. LAWRENCE COUNTY HISTORICAL ASSOCIATION – SILAS WRIGHT HOUSE/MUSEUM, 3 East Main Street, Canton. (315) 386-8133. **www.slcha.org**. Exhibits include: historic home of Silas Wright, Jr., New York State Governor from 1844-1846, period furnishings and changing exhibits on St. Lawrence County history. Hands-on history for kids.

SEAWAY TRAIL DISCOVERY CENTER, Ray & West Main Street, Sackets Harbor, (315) 646-1000, **www.seawaytrail.com**. Open May-October daily, 10am-5pm; November-April Tuesday-Saturday. Admission: $4 adults, $3 seniors, $2 children. Within the three stories of this 1817 Federal Style limestone building overlooking Lake Ontario you can "travel" the 454-mile Seaway Trail from a unique and majestic muraled orientation room, ride in a "fantasy car" or sit by a campsite. Houses a series of interactive kid-oriented exhibits exploring different aspects of the trail. Visit the 27 lighthouses of the Seaway Trail from the Maritime History room.

SCI-TECH CENTER OF NNY, 154 Stone Street, Watertown, (315) 788-1340, www.scitechcenter.org. Adults: $4.00, Children: $3.00, Seniors: $2.00, Family $14.00. A year-round, hands on museum of science and technology with more than 40 interactive exhibits.

STOCKHOLM HISTORICAL MUSEUM, Municipal Building, Winthrop, (315) 384-4764

THOUSAND ISLANDS ARTS CENTER AND HANDWEAVING MUSEUM, 314 John Street, Clayton, (315) 686-4123,www. tiartscenter.org. Houses a permanent textile collection and library, plus two studios dedicated to weaving and pottery. Mounts several yearly exhibits and maintains a year round arts curriculum. Open Monday through Friday, 9:00am – 5:00pm.

THOUSAND ISLANDS MUSEUM, 312 James Street, Clayton. (315) 686-5794. www.timuseum.org. Presents a modern gallery of permanent and rotating exhibits, along with a research library. Displays of older decoys and the Muskie Hall of Fame.

THE WILD CENTER, 45 Museum Drive, Tupper Lake. (518) 359-7800. Members, free. Age 4 and under, free, Youth (5-17) $15, Adult (18-64) $22, Senior/Military $20. Open daily during the summer season (May-October) and Fridays-Sundays during the winter. Check the official website for specific dates and hours of operation – **www.wildcenter.org**. A 115-acre indoor/outdoor natural history museum of epic proprtions. 54,000 square feet of exhibit space offers numerous hands-on activities as well as live exhibits including river otters, birds, amphibians and fish. "Animal Encounters" occur daily. Led by naturalists, these close-up sessions feature porcupines, owls, snakes and many other fascinating species. Walk through the iForest – an immersive sound experience, contemplative and calming. Outdoor exhibits take visitors into the ecosystems that surround the center, including Wild Walk, a trail across the treetops. Canoe and paddleboard trips are available on the river than runs through its campus, as well as daily guided trail walks. A hands-on place to get all kinds of new perspectives on the wild world of the Adirondacks. Plan to spend the day; a cafeteria with seating is available.

WHITE PINE CAMP, Paul Smiths, (518) 834-9328. www.whitepinecamp.com. An Adirondack "Great Camp" that served as the Summer White House for President Calvin Coolidge is open for public tours on Saturdays, July through Labor Day.

ALMANZO WILDER HOMESTEAD, 177 Stacy Road, Burke. (518) 483-1207 www.almanzowilderfarm.com. Opens for a summer season on Memorial Weekend. Home of Almanzo Wilder, subject of the book, Farmer Boy, written by his wife, Laura Ingalls Wilder. The site is on the National History Registry and is a Literary Landmark. The painstakingly restored homestead houses a wonderful collection of period artifacts, farm tools, Wilder photos, and plenty of information about the Wilders, Laura Ingalls, and farm life in the mid 19th century. Connect to the Farmer Boy story and to the way of life in 19th century rural northern New York.

ST. LAWRENCE POWER AND EQUIPMENT MUSEUM, 1755 State Highway 345, Madrid. (315) 344-7470. www.slpowermuseum.com. Seasonal – check website or call for hours. This outdoor museum's buildings, exhibits, and collections tell the story of the men and women who built, operated and traveled the North Country. Its mission, to preserve the power systems, equipment and related knowledge and skills that were integral to the development of the North Country, is accomplished through its many exhibit buildings: The Schoolhouse, The Blacksmith Shop, The Heritage Fibers Building, The Equine Pavillion, Saw and Shingle Mills, The Gas Station, The Farmhouse, The Collections Building, The Walker Granary, Big Engines and Equipment, The Log Cabin, The Cobbler Shop, The Antique Tractor Building, and The Carriage Barn. Added in 2020, Fort Tribute, a reconstructed Civil War era facility with stockade, barracks and headquarters, demonstrating Civil War garrison life. Major event is the Annual Old Fashioned Harvest Days Exhibition held in early September.

AKWESASNE CULTURAL CENTER MUSEUM, 321 Route 37, Hogansburg, (518) 358-2461, www.akwesasneculturalcenter.org
Tuesday through Friday, 9am-4pm. Weekend by appointment. Tells the story of Akwesasne through images, objects and interactives, and the unique history and culture of the Mohawk nation. Here one can find sweet grass baskets with such intricate design and weaving that they are masterpieces of art as well as function. The headdresses worn by chiefs of the different tribes of the six Iroquois nations show elaborate use of items such as splint wood, silver, brass, cloth, hawk and partridge feathers, and beads and quahog shells to create a sense of dignity and authority. A display of dolls without faces is a tribute to the belief that children could create their own characters depending on the mood they were experiencing. A diorama of a village with life centered in the long house helps one imagine a simpler life.

SIX NATIONS IROQUOIS CULTURAL CENTER
1462 County Route 60, Onchiota.
(518) 891-2299.
www.sixnationsindianmuseum.com

Open July-August, 10am-5pm, Tuesday through Sunday. This unique museum was built by the Fadden family and first opened in 1954. Its original two rooms have been expanded to four, reflecting the architecture of a traditional Long House. The floors are decorated with Haudenosaunee symbol and motif, the walls are laden with informative charts, beaded belts, paintings and other indigenous items of interest. 3000-plus artifacts with an emphasis on the culture of the Six Nations of the Iroquois Confederacy are presented from floor to ceiling.
The museum features storytelling lectures and a gift shop.

Explore The Wild Center's newly reinterpreted living wetland exhibit through the lens of the Thanksgiving Address, a Haudenosaunee (Six Nations/Iroquois) greeting that invites reflection on the ways our existence is interconnected with the natural world. Reimagined by artist and director of The Six Nations Indian Museum, David Fadden, this new experience will offer insight into the culture of the Indigenous Haudenosaunee people that have inhabited this region for thousands of years. Through the intersection of original art created by Fadden and storytelling videos, this new experience honors the ways of knowing our northern landscape.

Nature Trails

NATURE TRAILS, also see *Hiking Trails* Check out **www.northcountryguide.com** for other trail and hiking suggestions. And remember, many of the trails are for all seasons; hike in the spring, summer and fall and go in winter and take your skis or snowshoes.

ADIRONDACK PARK VISITOR INTERPRETIVE CENTER Route 30, one mile after the intersection with Route 86, Paul Smiths. (518) 37-6241. **www.northnet.org/adirondack.vic**. Information on ecology, diversity of the Adirondack Park nature exhibits, interactive displays, theater programs, interpretive trails and a butterfly house.

AUSABLE CHASM 2144, Route 9 Ausable Chasm. 800-537-1211. **www.ausablechasm.com**. Wonders, nature trails, scenic vistas and rafting.

GRASSE RIVER HERITAGE TRAIL ON COAKLEY ISLAND 2 Main Street in Canton begins by crossing the fully restored King Iron Bowstring Bridge. A short trail that winds through woods and features great river views, small waterfalls, resting benches, gristmill ruins and historical plaques. Across the highway, on Willow Island, is the Grasse River Sculpture Park, set on a grassy expanse with a tranquil river view. Within walking distance of downtown and parking is available at both sites. **www.grasseriverheritage.org**

MINNA ANTHONY COMMON NATURE CENTER 44927 Cross Road, Fineview. Exit 51 off I-81, Alexandria Bay. (315) 482-2479. Bird walks, guide hikes, canoe programs, trails, activities and evening concerts. Environmental educational visits.

REMINGTON RECREATION TRAIL Partridge Run Golf Course, Canton. (315) 386-4444. Paved 3.3 mile loop trail surrounding the golf course. Great for walking, biking and rollerblading.

ROBERT MOSES STATE PARK NATURE CENTER 32 Beach Marina Road, Massena. (315) 682-8663. Twelve miles of hiking/cross country trails; ski and snowshoe rentals available; nature walks, family programs offered daily in season. Children's day camps are offered during summer and school vacations with five rooms of interactive and live displays and exhibits. The Gift Shop features many hand-made items. Civil War Enactments and Festival of North Country Folk Life held every August. Performers and arts and crafts programs scheduled throughout the year. Hours: 8 a.m. - 8 p.m. during the summer; 8 a.m - 4:30 p.m. the rest of the year. Entrance fee to Nature Centre area: Free.

ST. LAWRENCE RECREATIONAL PATH 800-937-4748. www.cornwalltourism.com. For the outdoor enthusiast, this recreational path stretches over 70 kms, the majority of which follows the shoreline of the St. Lawrence River from Lancaster to Iroquois, Canada. Call for a free map.

SEAWAY TRAIL WALKS Waddington. For more information contact the Seaway Trail at 800-732-9298 or www.seawaytrail.com. St. Lawrence County's oldest church, industrial period houses made of native stone and the Ogden Land Office and among the historic register structures to be seen on the Seaway Trail Walks in the St. Lawrence Riverfront Village of Waddington, where the first machine made scythe and ax were made. Walks begin at the Town Hall, 38 Main Street, and are sponsored by the Waddington Chamber of Commerce. Cost is $8 rain or shine Walks begin at 5 p.m., run though October and last about one and a half hours.

WHITEFACE MOUNTAIN MEMORIAL HIGHWAY Wilmington (518) 946-7175 or 800-462-6236. wwwwhiteface.com It is 4,867 feet above sea level. Scenic eight mile toll road and an elevator to the summit. Daily 9 a.m. - 4 p.m. Through October, weather permitting.

NICANDRI NATURE CENTER 19 Robinson Bay Rd., Massena. (315) 705-5022 www.nicandrinaturecenter.org Nature comes alive at the Nicandri Nature Center! Built by the New York State Power Authority as a center for outdoor recreation and education for the community. The center combines nature and fun. Hike in the summer, ski and snowshoe in the winter and enjoy indoor programs all year round. Recreational activities include hiking, bird watching, skiing, snowshoeing and outdoor games. Groups' events include walking club, yoga, arts & crafts, turtle races, fish feeding, photography and much more. Open all year. Winter Wed.- Sun. 9-5; Summer Mon.-Wed. 9-5. Free Admission.

THE WILD CENTER 45 Museum Drive Tupper Lake (518) 359-7800. www.VisitWildCenter.org The Wild Center, formerly known as the Natural History Museum of the Adirondacks, is a natural history center in Tupper Lake, near the center of the New York State's Adirondack Park. The Wild Center is the only place in the Adirondacks designed specifically to connect you to nature in imaginative and engaging ways. The campus has miles of walking trails with river front access to guided canoe and stand up paddleboat trips, and a one of a kind elevated treetop experience called Wild Walk that takes you up and over a wild Adirondack forest. The Wild Center's main building contains 34,000 square feet of interactive exhibits, scores of live animals you can see up close, daily animal encounters, a giant interactive sphere called Planet Adirondack and much more.

The Wild Walk is a stunning aerial walkway across the treetops of a wild Adirondack forest. Walk up a trail of over 1,000 feet of bridges and experiences to the treetops of the Adirondack forest. Visit a four story twig tree house, swing over on bridges, clamber over a spider's web or climb to a full sized bald eagle's nest 40 feet off the ground at the highest point. Frequent pop-up programs led by the staff allow the discovery first-hand what makes the Adirondacks such a unique place.

The Hall of the Adirondacks provides time to spend with a myriad of fish, turtles, and other animals and plant species to get a deeper understanding and appreciation for the inner workings of nature in this unique region. Explore the trails of the 115 acre campus on your own or with one of the guided Naturalist walks. Everyday the Naturalists bring animals into the Big Wolf Great Hall for animal encounters. Great for all ages, these close up sessions feature porcupines, owls, snakes and many other fascinating species.

Plane Rides

In the Adirondacks, our mountain, streams and scenic roadways offer some of the prettiest views and panoramic vistas found in the six million acre Adirondack Park. Charming towns and villages provide a variety of unique attractions from community festivals to open air theatrical productions. In summer, fresh seasonal roadside stands offering homemade rustic goods to locally produced honey. Fall and winter bring colourful landscapes and festivals celebrating holidays and winter sports. Every season brings unique views and experiences. Spring bursts wildflowers while the warmth of summer offers bountiful beauty.

ADIRONDACK FLYING SERVICE
27 Airplane Lane, Lake Placid.
(518) 523-2473. www.flyawayanywhere.com "You'll never experience the Adirondacks like this." Scenic flights take off from the Lake Placid airport just on the edge of the village. Choose the 20 minute scenic tour featuring Olympic Village, the High Peaks and the lakes, or choose a special events flights. Each 20 minute flight offers a unique perspective of this amazing park.

HELMS AERO SERVICE Rt. 30, Long Lake. (518) 624-3931. An incredible bird's eye view of the 6 million acres of the Adirondack Park. Experienced pilots navigate and tell you the history of the Adirondacks.

Seaplane Rides

INLET BIRD SEAPLANE (315) 357-3631.

PAYNE'S AIR SERVICE (315) 357-3971. There are several seaplane operators. Take the opportunity to see the beautiful Adirondack Mountains from a "bird's eye view." There are so many lakes in the area you'll have trouble courting them. Go on a short ride or arrange to go for a longer excursion.

1000 ISLANDS AIR 101A South Street, Gananoque Waterfront, Ontario, Canada. (613) 382-7111. www.islandair.ca. Treat yourself to an aerial view of the spectacular 1000 Islands. See the island estates and Boldt Castle. May1- October 31, Daylight - Dark

1000 ISLANDS AVIATION SERVICES
Maxson Airfield, 23820 NYS Rt. 26, Alexandria Bay. (315) 482-4024. A 4,300 foot General Aviation airport is the heart of the Thousand Islands region. Scenic air tours, flight training and aircraft parking, storage and maintenance. Year Round 8 a.m. - Sunset.

Private Campgrounds

4-H CAMP OVERLOOK
70 Beach Road, Mountain View
(518) 379-9192
www.4hcampoverlook.org

1000 ISLANDS CAMPGROUND
42099 Route 12, Alexandria Bay
(315) 686-2600, Open May – October
www.1000islandscampground.com

BABBLING BROOK RV PARK
1623 County Route 4, Fort Covington
(518) 358-4245
Open May 1 to October 15
www.babblingbrookrvpark.com

**BACK BAY CAMPGROUND
AND COTTAGES**
302 Chapman Point, Hammond
(315) 324-5612
www.backbaycamping.com

BIRCH HAVEN CAMPGROUND
38191 Route 12 East, Clayton
(315) 686-5253
Open May – October
www.birchhavencamp.com

BIRD'S NEST CAMPGROUND
2989 County Route 6, Hammond
(315) 375-8524

BLAKE MCNEIL CAMPSITE
20 Pike Street, South Colton
(315) 262-2640

BLEVIN'S CAMPSITE
104 River Lane, Ogdensburg
(315) 393-4484

BUTTERNUT COVE COTTAGES
2538A County Route 6, Hammond
(315) 778-4022
www.butternutcovecottages.com

CAMP CAROL CAMPS
4014 County Route 6, Hammond
(315) 375-6637
www.campcarolny.com

CAMPER VILLAGE CAMPSITE
7036 State Highway 3, Cranberry Lake
(315) 848-2501

CARRY FALLS/PARMENTER SITE
Carry Falls Reservoir, Brookfield Power
Carry Falls Road, South Colton
(315) 262-2640, Open May to September

CATAMOUNT LODGE AND FOREST LLC
2092 State Highway 56, Colton
(315) 262-2555
www.catamountlodge.com

**CHARLIE'S INN AND JUNCTION
CAMPGROUND**
44 Junction Road, Lake Clear
(518) 891-9858

DASHNAW CAMP WILDWOOD
193 Mitchell Road, Heuvelton
(315) 578-2302
www.campwildwoodny.com

DEER RIVER CAMPSITE
123 Deer River Drive, Malone
(518) 483-0060

DONALDSON'S CAMPSITE
4426 State Route 30, Lake Clear
(518) 891-4070

**FRENCH CREEK MARINA
AND CAMPGROUND**
250 Wahl Street, Clayton
(315) 686-3621, Open April – October
www.frenchcreekmarina.com

HIGH FALLS PARK CAMPGROUND
34 Cemetery Road, Chateaugay
(518) 497-3156
www.highfallsparkcampground.com

HILLSIDE CAMPGROUNDS
15 Smith Drive, Massena
(315) 769-5403

HOUMIEL'S CAMPSITE
State Highway 37, Ogdensburg
(315) 393-4936

JELLYBEAN'S CAMPGROUND
7 St. Regis Street, Brasher Falls
(315) 389-4771
www.riversidecampgroundny.com

LANZ'S MOTEL, COTTAGES AND RV CAMPGROUND
40033 Route 12, Clayton, (315) 686-5690

LISBON TOWN CAMPGROUND
9975 NY Route 37, Ogdensburg
(315) 393-5374 www.townoflisbonny.org

LOG CABINS AND CAMPGROUNDS
3114 County Route 6, Hammond
(315) 375-6691

LYDIA'S PLACE, INC. RV CAMPSITE
260 Lake Ozonia Road, Hopkinton
(315) 261-2559 www.lydiasplacerv.com

MASSAQUAPI CABINS AND CAMPS
2380 County Route 6, Hammond
(315) 324-5524

MASSENA INTERNATIONAL KAMPGROUND-COTTAGES
84 County Route 42 Extension
Massena, (315) 769-9483
www.massenainternationalkampground.com

MCLEAR'S COTTAGE COLONY AND CAMPGROUND
2477 County Route 6, Hammond
(315) 375-6508, **www.mclears.com**

MERRY KNOLL 1000 ISLANDS CAMPGROUND
38115 State Route 12 East, Clayton
(315) 686-3055, Open May – October
www.merryknollcampground.com

NATURAL BRIDGE KOA
6081 NY Route 3, Natural Bridge
(315) 644-4098 **www.koa.com**

NORTH COUNTRY COTTAGES
26228 County Route 6,
Hammond
(315) 375-4671

PINE RIDGE PARK CAMPSITE
212 State Route 122, Constable
(518) 358-4125

PLEASANT VIEW COTTAGES AND CAMPS
2626 County Route 6, Hammond
(315) 375-6736

PONDEROSA CAMPSITES
417 Ponderosa Road, Chateaugay
(518) 497-6430
www.ponderosacampsite.com

RAINBOW FALLS POND
Brookfield Power, Exit off Route 56 at bridge in South Colton, 13687

RIVER LANE CAMPGROUND
104 River Lane, Ogdensburg
(253) 922-0980

RIVERSIDE ACRES CAMPGROUND AND COTTAGES
38241 Route 12 East, Clayton
(315) 686-4001
www.riversideacrescampgrounds.com

ST. REGIS FALLS SCENIC CAMPSITE
19 Water Street, St. Regis Falls
(518) 856-9821 www.campnative.com

STARK FALLS POND Brookfield Power
Off Route 56 at Joe Indian Road turn
South Colton, 13687

STOWE BAY CAMPGROUND
78 Stowe Bay Road, Colton
(315) 262-2257

SWAN BAY RESORT
43615 Route 12, Alexandria Bay
(315) 482-SWAN, Open May – October
www.swanbayresort.com

There are also several campgrounds located in the provinces of Ontario and Quebec in Canada. These are some websites with more information about camping across the border. National Parks: **www.pc.gc.ca**

Public Concerts

Potsdam is considered the cultural center of the North Country, as it is home to SUNY Potsdam's nationally renowned Crane School of Music, which offers a concert, play or recital nearly every day during the academic year.

NORWOOD VILLAGE GREEN CONCERT SERIES *Northern New York State's Premier Outdoor Concert Series* Over the past two and a half decades The Series has provided residents and visitors alike with music from Grammy, Juno and Emmy award winners as well as a host of international, national and regional performers in this family-oriented, community-based setting. The Series prides itself on providing programming for children and youth and has a long history of providing opportunities to student musicians. Most concerts are held in Norwood's Liotta Village Green Band Shell. Admission is free. www.business.visitslc.com (315) 353-2437

COMMUNITY PERFORMANCE SERIES IN RESIDENCE AT SUNY POTSDAM Office and box office located in the Performing Arts Center at SUNY Potsdam, 44 Pierrepont Avenue, Potsdam. *The Guest Artist Series* is geared toward adults, and the *Meet the Arts* performances are geared toward children. Ticket prices vary. Schedule and reservation information available on-line at www.cpspotsdam.org or by calling (315) 267-2277

SUNY POTSDAM'S CRANE SCHOOL OF MUSIC Student ensemble performances as well as faculty and student recitals are open to the public. Most are free-of-charge, including the popular *Crane Candlelight Concert*. Most concerts are located in either Snell Music Theatre or Hosmer Concert Hall. Schedule of performances listed on-line at www.cpspotsdam.org (315) 267-2775

ST. LAWRENCE UNIVERSITY Performances by faculty and students are open to the public, including concerts by the Laurentian Singers. Calendar of Events listed online at www.stlawu.edu or by calling (315) 229-5166

OGDENSBURG COMMAND PERFORMANCE SERIES Presenting professional touring productions and providing educational opportunities to foster a greater understanding of the performing arts. Offers a Youtheatre: Class Acts program in conjunction with local schools. Performances in George Hall Auditorium at Ogdensburg Free Academy at 1100 State Street in Ogdensburg Schedule and ticket prices on-line at www.ilovetheatre.org (315) 393-2625

PICKENS HALL AND OPERA HOUSE Providing family entertainment through a variety of musical styles, educational opportunities and lifestyle classes. Located in Pickens General Store offering Amish crafts, cheese and chocolates, at 83 North State Street Heuvelton. Schedule and ticket prices available at www.pickenshall.com or by calling (315) 344-7050

Rafting Trips

ADIRONDACK RIVER OUTFITTERS, INC. Guided rafting adventures on the Black River, Hudson River and Moose River, May - Oct., Daily. 140 Newell Street Watertown and 4511 State Route 28 in North River. www.aroadventures.com (315) 788-2297 or 800-525-7238.

ADIRONDAC RAFTING COMPANY, Lake Placid, (518) 523-1635, www.adirondacrafting.com (Note: The company spells its name without a "k" after the word Adirondack.)

HUDSON RIVER RAFTING CO., 1 Main Street in North Creek. World-class rafting, offering full-day and shorter trips. Spring/Fall weekends. www.hudsonriverrafting.com 800-888-RAFT

WHITEWATER CHALLENGERS, INC., Operating on the Salmon, Hudson, Moose & Black Rivers (April - October). Class III - IV. May - Oct., call for schedule. 16129 Foster Park Rd., Dexter www.whitewaterchallengers.com. 800-443-RAFT.

Road Biking

MORLEY-BUCKS BRIDGE-WEST POTSDAM LOOP A 22 mile moderate loop, that takes you along the Grasse River through Morley to Bucks Bridge, then to West Potsdam and back to Canton through prime farmland.

OLD MILL TOWN LOOP A 31 mile moderate loop through the towns of Canton and Potsdam, with visible mill ruins in the hamlet of Pyrites as a highlight.

LAMPSON FALLS LOOP A 45 mile difficult loop through Canton, Clare, Pierrepont and Russell with a stop at scenic Lampson Falls.

PYRITES-OLD DEKALB ROAD A 16 mile difficult loop taking the rider into a series of scenic hills south and west of Canton.

INDIAN CREEK TOUR A 25 mile moderate loop taking the rider along flat to gently rolling country roads between Canton, Morley and Rensselaer Falls and completely around the Indian Creek Nature Center.

ROUTE 30, MALONE TO TUPPER LAKE is 60 miles of wide (6 feet in most places) shoulders and light traffic. Stop for a picnic and swim at Meacham Lake.

Resources:
www.bikethebyways.org – biking the scenic byways of the Adirondack North Country

www.STLCtrails.com – detailed directions with trail maps for cycling routes and mountain biking trails.
Traillink.com – by Rails-to-Trails Conservancy

Groups:

ADIRONDACK MOUNTAIN CLUB – LAURENTIAN CHAPTER – scheduled outings (including biking) throughout the year. Membership is not required to participate and there is no charge. Their events calendar can be accessed at www.adklaurentian.org

CGSW RACING, OGDENSBURG – hold several events for cycling including Mini Maple Kids Triathlon, held annually in August. Find them on FaceBook

FRIENDS OF HIGLEY – "THE HIGLEY 100" - annual 100km century ride held in early September. Rides begin and end at Higley Trails Lodge in Higley Flow State Park, South Colton. There is also a 50k half century ride as well as shorter loops ranging from 2 to 25 miles which family and friends may enjoy while their century riders are on course.

Scuba Diving

The St. Lawrence River, lying between the United States and Canada, holds numerous popular dive destinations, including many beautifully preserved historical and recent shipwrecks. Visibility in the river is generally very good with depths >100 feet.

An overview of the wrecks accessible to scuba divers can be found at these two websites: www.1000islands.com or www.shipwreckexpo.com

Local Dive Shops

BLUE FIN DIVING
4701 State Highway 68, Ogdensburg. (315) 344-4064. PADI 5-star dive shop. Full-service dive center; charters, rentals, sales, service, instruction and air and Nitrox fills. www.bluefindiving.net

HUNT'S DIVE SHOP
48702 Route 12, Clayton. (315) 686-1070 or (315) 788-2075. Full-service dive center; charters, rentals, sales, service, instruction, air and Nitrox fills.
www.huntsdiveshop.net

THOUSAND ISLANDS DIVE EXCURSIONS
834 Rees St., Clayton (315) 686-5542
www.divetide.com

BLUE FOOT DIVING RECREATIONS AND TECHNICAL DIVE CHARTERS.
Marina at Keewaydin State Park in Alexandria Bay. www.bluefootdiving.com

Diving in Canada

ABUCS SCUBA CHARTERS
12 Water Street East, Brockville Ontario, Canada, Rentals and Nitrox on site.
www.divebrockville.com

Shipwrecks

For more information on shipwrecks in the northern New York region, visit **www.sonarguy.com/st-lawrence-river** and **www.1000islands.com/sunken-treasures-the-wrecks-of-the-1000-islands**. A few of these shipwrecks are listed on these websites.

SHIP: EASTCLIFFE HALL
History: This steel freighter weighing 3.335 tons and 343 ft. long struck a shoal at 4 a.m. on July 14, 1970 while carrying a load of "pig iron." It sank within minutes and nine lives were lost. There were 12 survivors.
Location: Approximately 3/4 mile south of Crysler Marina, at Upper Canada Village, Morrisburg, Ontario between Morrisburg, Ontario and Cornwall, Ontario (across the border from Ogdensburg, NY and Massena, NY).

SHIP: CONESTOGA
History: This 2,008-ton ship with a double planked propeller was capable of doing 8 knots per mile. Launched on July 6, 1878, it sank on May 22, 1922. The Conestoga lies in about 30 feet of water and has a quick current. This ship is used by many visitors as a site for night diving. Location: Conestoga lies alongside the old canal wall a short distance west of Cardinal, Ontario. On the north shore of the St. Lawrence and only a few miles east of the International Bridge at Ogdensburg, NY.

SHIP: FLEURMARIE
History: This Brigantine was built in 1850 at lanoraie, Quebec. It was listed as 155.6 tons, 92.5 ft. x 20 ft. x 8.7 ft. with a square stem. This ship had deteriorated while sitting at dock in Prescott, Ontario, and after a fire on board it was sunk in the mid channel and now rests on a rock/sand bottom at 52 ft. below water where she is surrounded by a quick surface current. Location: South of the "windmill" the site lies on the American side east of Ogdensburg and west from buoy 131B.

SHIP: AMERICA
History: On June 20, 1932 this steel oil barge was sunk due to an explosion. The shoal's side gives evidence to the America's work with the blasted rock rubble alongside.
Location: At a depth of 75 ft., the America rests upside down across the shipping channel from Singer Castle and Dark Island. Normally a guide-line is buoyed immediately east of Black Buoy # 167 on the downstream side of the shipping lane.

VESSEL: LOWBLAW'S
History: This wooden hull sits off Ogdensburg's waterfront about 52 ft. depth with a noticeable current. The vessel is about 130 ft. x 24 ft. x 8 ft. with some decking remaining. Visits to this site are by boat. The wreckage appears burnt to the water line but sits about 8 ft. high on a firm clay-silt bottom.
Location: This site sits directly in front of the large brick chimney on the Ogdensburg shore and south of the downstream channel.

Sledding

With an average snowfall topping 100 inches per year the North Country is the perfect playground for winter sports of all kinds. Family friendly snow tubing has grown in popularity in the recent years, attracting riders of all ages looking for an adrenaline rush.

TUBING HILL AT TITUS MOUNTAIN
215 John Road, Malone
www.titusmountain.com
The multi lane tubing pull includes an 880 feet run with a vertical drop which will push riders to a speed above 20 mph. A tow line carries riders to the top of the mountain.

MAPLE RIDGE SNOW PARK 7421 East Road, Lowville. Maple Ridge Snow Park is the largest snow tubing hill in Northern New York. It has more than 8 lanes that are over 1200 feet long and with over 100' vertical drop. Enjoy spectacular views of the Black River and Adirondacks as you summit the mountain on the tube tow and as it pulls you back up the hill. The warming barn is complete with a concession stand, seating and game table. Operating hours Sat, Sun and School Holidays 12 -4. Cost: Age 16 and under $12; Age 17+ $15

DRY HILL SKI AREA 23682 Cty Rt. 67, Watertown. **www.skidryhill.com**
This family friendly ski center offers tubing on Fridays nights and all day Saturday and Sunday. Warm up afterwards in the Fireside Lounge.

Two great sledding hills can be found on the SUNY Canton campus and Clarkson campus. Call their switchboards for direction.

Snowmobiling

Information on snowmobiling in the North Country, including contact information on how to join a club, is available through the New York State Snowmobilers Association at PO Box 740, Central Square, New York 13036, Phone 888-624-3849.

More than 500 miles of groomed trails in St. Lawrence County are maintained by the St. Lawrence County Snowmobile Association. Snowmobiling may begin after the big game hunting season usually in the beginning of December and running through April. The club's website is at www.slcsa.org and includes information about membership as well as trail conditions and special events that may be happening. A trail map can also be requested through the club, or the St. Lawrence County Chamber of Commerce, which also includes snowmobiling information on their website at **www.stlctrails.com**
There are designated and marked trails within St. Lawrence County and others that are only useable with the permission of the landowner. Please be respectful of these trails and also if the trails are for

dual purposes such as cross-country skiing keep a lookout for other people and sleds. Many of the county trails connect into the regional trails of the Adirondacks near Cranberry Lake, Piercefield and Childwold. There are a number of local businesses which are popular stops both for fueling up the sled and the riders.

0ver 4,000 snowmobiles are registered in St. Lawrence County, and thousands of visitors travel here from throughout the North East and Canada each year to participate in this most popular of sports. Special events are hosted by local snowmobile clubs, and it is not unusual to hear the whine of engines on a sunny winter day as sleds go zipping by on their way to poker runs, club meets, and races. Detailed maps are available from the Snowmobile Association for a small fee.

Snowmobile/Trail Conditions

INDIAN LAKE SNOWMOBILE CONDITIONS (518) 648-5112 www.ilsnow.com

INDIAN LAKE SKILL HILL (518) 648-5611 or (518) 648-5828.

INLET SNOWMOBILE TRAIL CONDITIONS 1-866-GO-INLET.

INLET CROSS COUNTRY SKIING TRAIL CONDITIONS 1-866-GO-INLET

LONG LAKE AND RAQUETTE LAKE SNOWMOBILE TRAIL CONDITIONS (518) 624-3941. www.longlake-ny.com

MCCAULEY MOUNTAIN SKI AREA (315) 369-3225.

OLD FORGE/TOWN OF WEBB SNOWMOBILE TRAIL CONDITIONS (315) 369-6983

Local Clubs in and Around St. Lawrence County

BOONDOCKERS, RUSSELL 172 Dean Road, Russell (315) 386-2301 www.slcsa.org/clubs/boondockers

PARISHVILLE PACEMAKERS 2787 White Hill Road, Parishville, NY 13672, (315) 265-0898

CHILDWOLD SNOPACKERS (315) 699-8198. PO Box 55, Childwold, 12922. www.slcsa.org/clubs/childwold-snopackers

COLTON SNO SKIPPERS PO Box 536, South Colton (315) 212-0070 www.slcsa.org/clubs/colton-sno-skipper-inc

CRANBERRY LAKE MOUNTAINEERS PO Box 481, Cranberry Lake (315) 848-8835. www.slcsa.org/clubs/cranberry-lake-mountaineers

DAIRYLAND SNOWMOBILE CLUB 1039 Sand Street Road, Brier Hill, 13614 (315) 528-0166 www.slcsa.org/clubs/dairyland-snowmobile-club

EDWARDS SNOWMOBILE CLUB (315) 562-2320. 214 Talcville Road, Edwards, 13635. www.slcsa.org/clubs/edwards-snowmobile-club

GRASSE RIVER GROOMERS 330 County Route 14, Madrid 13660 (315) 322-4041 www.slcsa.org/clubs/grasse-river-groomers

HERMON SLEDDERS 1248 County Route 20, Dekalb Junction, 13630 (315) 347-1779 www.slcsa.org/clubs/hermon-sledders.

HEUVELTON PUNCHLOCK TRAVELERS (315) 393-1151. PO Box 198, Heuvelton, 13654. www.slcsa.org/clubs/heuvelton-punchlock-travelers

TRI TOWN TRAILBLAZERS PO Box 98, Helena, 13649 (315) 769-2195 www.slcsa.org/clubs/tri-tow-trailblazers

MOONLIGHTER'S SNOWMOBILE CLUB SUPPORTING LONG LAKE AND RAQUETTE LAKE TRAILS AND EVENTS Town of Long Lake, Long Lake, NY 12847, (518) 624-3077. www.mylonglake.com/moonlighters-snowmobile-club

Snowshoeing

FOR A MAP of some of the best snowshoeing trails in St. Lawrence County, visit the St. Lawrence County Chamber of Commerce web site www.stlctrails.com

Snowshoeing is a great way for the whole family to enjoy our beautiful North Country winters – and it's great exercise too! While you can snowshoe almost anywhere, many trails in the area are groomed for snowshoeing and cross-country skiing.

Here is a sampling of the best trails in the northern New York area:

Brasher State Forest off County Road 50, Brasher Falls, or Route 11 at St. Lawrence Central School. www.dec.ny.gov

Catamount Forest 9 miles south of South Colton on the east side of State Route 56. Limited parking available at Catamount Mountain trailhead, just south of the lodge driveway. Groomed trails open to the public, **www.catamountlodge.com**

Cranberry Lake Area, The Five Ponds Wilderness Area, southwest of Cranberry Lake is one of the most remote and least-used areas of New York State. Details and maps are available at the New York State DEC website at **www.dec.ny.gov**

If you are looking for a guided adventure contact the Cranberry Lake Guide Service or Packbasket Adventures found at **www.northcountryguide.com.**
Fort Jackson State Forest, Town of Stockholm. **www.dec.ny.gov**

Higley Flow State Park Off Route 56, two miles east of South Colton. A variety of trails are offered for snowshoeing and cross-country skiing. There is a trail register located adjacent to the parking lot which snowshoers and skiers are asked to sign in to keep a record of trail usage. Trail Information and map available. (315) 262-2880.

High Flats State Forest Parishville, from County Road 58, right on Rodwell Mill Road, left jog to Crowley Road, 4.5 miles of trails, 2.6 miles of unplowed road used to complete the loop. www.dec.ny.gov.

Postwood Park and County Forest Hannawa Falls, 4 miles south of Potsdam. The main trail starts at Postwood Park parking lot and is comprised of two loops. The first and smaller, 1.6 mile loop is located on the west side of the River Road. The other loop is located on the east side of the River Road and runs for an approximate distance of 4.1 miles.

The Robert Moses State Park, located off State Highway 37, three miles north of Massena offers 15.5 miles (25k) of trail, as well as ski and snowshoe rentals.

The local colleges at SUNY Potsdam Lehman Park, 2.5 miles (4k) of trails located off State Highway 56; Clarkson University, located off State Highway 11 offers 5 miles (8k); and SUNY Canton, located off State Highway 68, offers 9.3 miles (15k) accessed from parking lot No. 6 across from French Hall {bear Left at the Y).

The Remington Recreation Center at Partridge Run Golf Course and St. Lawrence University Golf and Country Club, both located in Canton, have groomed trails.

St. Lawrence State Park Golf Course, 4955 State Highway 37, Ogdensburg
www.dec.ny.gov

The Upper and Lower Lakes Wildlife Management Area: Indian Creek Nature Center, in Rensselaer Falls, offers 5 miles (8k) of trails. And for the rugged survivalist, check out the Five Ponds Wilderness Area southwest of Cranberry Lake. This is suitable for people who carry and know how to use field repair materials and survival equipment. There are about 40 miles of trails here. The starting point is in the Village of Wanakena, two miles south of State Highway 3.

Special Tours

The St. Lawrence Seaway & Power Project- In the mid 1950s, one of the most ambitious public work projects in North America was developed on the U. S. -Canada border at Massena. The Robert Moses-Robert Saunders Power Project harnessed the awesome power of the St. Lawrence River's International Rapids for hydroelectric production. But providing inexpensive power for Alcoa, Reynolds Metals and General Motors plants was only part of the story. The power dam between Barnhart Island and Cornwall, Ontario, also created a deep water pool necessary for the construction of the St. Lawrence Seaway... the long dreamed-of "fourth coast" that would allow ocean-going vessels to sail from the Atlantic into the Great Lakes and the North American heartland. The power project, jointly operated by the New York Power Authority and Ontario Hydro produced the first power in 1958, while Seaway construction finished a year later.

THE DWIGHT D. EISENHOWER LOCK VISITOR CENTER in Massena gives visitors an up close look at the operation of one of two mammoth lock chambers maintained by the U.S. St. Lawrence Seaway Development Corporation. Here visitors get a bird's eye view as ships up to 760 feet long are raised or lowered over 40 feet in about 10 minutes.

The Visitor's Center also features a gift shop, concession area and displays. A display on the New York Power Authority dam can be seen at the Seaway Visitor's Center.

In addition, a wonderful panoramic view of the powerhouse can be seen at nearby Hawkins Point, the future home of the new Power Authority Visitor's Center.

ST. LAWRENCE-FDR POWER PROJECT VISITOR'S CENTER
800 Barnhart Island Rd, Massena NY. (315) 764-0226 ext. 304 or 800-262-6972. Memorial Day - Labor Day, daily 9:30 a.m. -6 p.m.. Labor Day - Columbus Day, daily 9 a.m. 4:30 p.m. Columbus Day - Memorial Day, Monday - Friday 9 a.m. -4:30 p.m. Free. www.nyps.gov

The heart of St. Lawrence-FDR Power Project is the Robert Moses-Robert H. Saunders Power Dam which first generated power in 1958. It is one of North America's largest- and most economical- power producers. The entire project encompasses over 37 miles of the St. Lawrence River Valley and includes two control dams and three huge locks used by ocean-going cargo ships and tankers. The visitor's centre at the power dam features state - of - the art exhibits on energy, electricity and the area's history. Learn how the power dam and the St. Lawrence Seaway were built, in what was one of the largest construction projects of its type in the world.

From the Dwight D. Eisenhower Lock Viewing Deck and Visitor's Center you can watch huge tankers and ships being lifted or lowered 42 feet in the lock chamber. A parking area on the north side of the lock provides a vantage point when the viewing deck is closed. Call ahead to determine when ships will be arriving at the locks. (315) 769-2422.

1000 ISLAND SKYDECKS
Lansdowne,
Ontario, KE01LO
(613) 659-2335
www.1000islandsskydeckcom.
Spectacular view of the 1000 Islands and St. Lawrence River from the observation deck. Open 7 days a week, mid April though October. Located between the spans of the Thousand Islands International Bridge and Hill Island.

SUNFEATHER SOAP FACTORY TOURS
1151 St. Hwy. 72 Parishville, NY.
(315) 265-3648.
wwwsunsoap.com.
Sunfeather Natural Soap Co. is the oldest and largest cold process soap factory in the United States. Sunfeather produces over 150 different types of soap which are shipped worldwide.

The company has gained international acclaim since the business first began in Sandy Maine's farmhouse kitchen in 1979. The company's inventory includes more than 250 kinds of soap and related products- from a best-selling line of women's floral soaps and eco-friendly bulk soaps to the award-winning Washy Squashy Modeling Soap for kids.

Visit the soap museum and see the multimedia presentation on essential oils, perfumery and aroma therapy.

Tours by appointment. Groups rates available.

ADIRONDACK FRAGRANCE AND FLAVOR FARM
1151 NY-72, Potsdam; (315) 265-1176
Unique Adirondack homemade soap, cologne, herbal bug repellents, gentle high quality items. The farm develops fragrances and flavor products that relate to the history, flora, fauna and landscapes of Northern New York.
 Open 8-4 Mon-Fri; 10-4 Sat.

Speedboat Rides

Bring back the Roaring 20s with a speedboat ride around many of the islands.

The triple cockpit runabout holds six people. The third cockpit on the 1929 reproduction craft is like a rumble seat and lets passengers feel the wind and the spray. The mahogany boat is similar to ones on display in the museum. Free for children younger than 5.

THE ANTIQUE BOAT MUSEUM SPEEDBOAT RIDES
 750 Mary St., Clayton
(315) 686-4104
www.abm.org

State Campgrounds

ALDRICH POND WILD FOREST
Towns of Pitcairn, Fine and Webb
Contact: New York State Department of Conservation
190 Outer Main Street, Potsdam
(315) 265-3090
www.dec.ny.gov
Open year-round

AU SABLE POINT CAMPGROUND
3346 Lake Shore Road, Peru
(518) 561-7080

BOG RIVER COMPLEX (Including Horseshoe Lake, Eastern Five Ponds Access Primitive Area, Lows Lake and Big Tupper/Piercefield Flow Conservation Area)
Located in the towns of Long Lake, Tupper Lake, Clifton, Colton and Piercefield
Contact: New York State Department of Conservation
190 Outer Main Street, Potsdam
(315) 265-3090
www.dec.ny.gov
Open year-round

BUCK POND CAMPGROUND AND DAY USE AREA
1339 County Route 60
Onchiota

CRANBERRY LAKE CAMPGROUND
230 Lone Pine Road, Cranberry Lake
(315) 848-2315
Open mid-May through September

CRANBERRY LAKE COMPLEX (Cranberry Lake Wild Forest, Conifer-Emporium Conservation Easement and Massawepie Conservation Easement)
Contact for this area: New York State Department of Conservation
190 Outer Main Street, Potsdam
(315) 265-3090
www.dec.ny.gov

FISH CREEK POND
4523 NY Route 30, Saranac Lake
(518) 891-4560
Open May through October

MEADOWBROOK CAMPGROUND AND DAY USE AREA
1174 NYS Route 86, Ray Brook
(518) 891-4351
Open mid-May until September

MEACHAM LAKE CAMPGROUND
119 State Camp Road, Malone
(518) 483-5116
Open mid-May through September

ROLLINS POND CAMPGROUND
4523 NY Route 30, Saranac Lake
(518) 891-3239
Open mid-May until mid-September

SARANAC LAKE ISLANDS
4468 State Route 3, Saranac Lake
(518) 891-1309

TAYLOR POND CAMPGROUND AND DAY USE AREA
1865 Silver Lake Road, Ausable Forks
(518) 647-5250
Open mid-May until September

WILMINGTON NOTCH CAMPGROUND AND DAY USE AREA
4953 NYS Route 86, Wilmington
(518) 946-7172
Open May until mid- October

Did You Know?

It is illegal in New York State to transport untreated firewood more than 50 miles from its origin. By transporting firewood, you could be spreading diseases and invasive insects. When transporting firewood, you must carry proof of source (receipt from a vendor), origin (self-issued certificate from DEC website) or treatment (label indicating treatment method). Failure to do so may result in you being ticketed and subject to a fine. Many times firewood is available near the park or campground.

State Parks

New York State offers a variety of beautiful parks for camping. Many are located on bodies of water to provide opportunities for boating, fishing and swimming.

The parks in northern New York are listed along with the amenities and activities available. Reservations can be made from 1 day to 9 months in advance by calling toll free 1-800-456-CAMP or **www.newyorkstateparks.reserveamerica.com**

You can save 15 – 20% by reserving a weeknight (Sunday – Thursday) campsite! For spur of the moment trips, some rentals are available on a walk-up basis.

New York State Department of Conservation also has many campsites in northern New York. These sites tend to be more rustic to provide a more primitive camping experience.

BURNHAM POINT STATE PARK
340765 NY Route 12E
Cape Vincent
(315) 654-2522
Open mid- May to Labor Day

Amenities: boat launches, campsites, dockage, dumping stations, grills, pavilions, picnic tables, playgrounds, powerboats, showers, tent/trailer sites

Activities: fishing, hunting

CANOE-PICNIC POINT STATE PARK
36661 Cedar Point State Park Drive
Clayton
(315) 654-2522
Open during the summer

Amenities: only reachable by boat, cabins, campsites, dockage, grills, nature trails, pavilions, picnic tables, powerboats, showers

Activities: fishing, hiking, hunting

CEDAR POINT STATE PARK
36661 Cedar Point State Park Drive
Clayton
(315) 654-2522
Open Memorial Day until Labor Day

Amenities: cabins, campsites, dockage, grills, nature trails, pavilions, picnic tables, powerboats, showers

Activities: fishing, hiking, hunting

CEDAR ISLAND STATE PARK
County Route 93
Hammond
(315) 783-1963
Open Memorial Day until Labor Day

Amenities: boat dockage, campsites, grills, pavilions, picnic tables, powerboats

Activities: fishing, hunting

COLES CREEK STATE PARK
Route 37, Waddington
(315) 388-5636
Open mid-May until around Columbus Day

Amenities: boat launches, campsites, dockage, dumping stations, grills, marina, pavilions, picnic tables, playgrounds, powerboats, showers, swimming beach, tent/trailer sites

Activities: fishing, hunting, recreation programs

CUMBERLAND BAY STATE PARK
152 Cumberland Head Road
Plattsburgh
5118-563-5240
Open early May to Columbus Day

Amenities: campsites, dumping stations, food, grills, pavilions, picnic tables, playgrounds, playing fields, showers, swimming beach, tent/trailer sites

DEWOLF POINT STATE PARK
45920 County Route 191
Fineview (Wellesley Island)
(315) 482-2012
Open mid-May until mid-September

Amenities: boat launches, cabins, campsites, dockage, grills, pavilions, picnic tables, power boats, showers, tent/trailer sites

Activities: fishing, ice fishing

**EEL WEIR
STATE PARK**
County Road 79
Ogdensburg
(315) 393-1138
Open Memorial Day through Labor Day
Amenities: boat launches, campsites, grills, pavilions, picnic tables, showers, tent/trailer sites
Activities: fishing

**GRASS POINT
STATE PARK**
42247 Grassy Point Road
Alexandria Bay
(315) 686-4472
Open mid-May through mid-September
Amenities: boat launches, boat rentals, campsites, cottages, dockage, dumping stations, grills, pavilions, picnic tables, playgrounds, powerboats, showers, swimming beach, tent/trailer sites
Activities: fishing, hunting

**HIGLEY FLOW
STATE PARK**
442 Cold Brook Drive
Colton
(315) 262-2880
Open from Memorial Day until Labor Day
Amenities: boat launches, camper recreation, campsites, dumping stations, grills, museum/visitor center, nature trails, pavilions, picnic tables, playgrounds, powerboats, showers, swimming beach, tent/trailer sites
Activities: fishing, hiking, hunting, ice fishing, recreation programs, snowmobiling, snowshoeing trails, X-country skiing

**JACQUES CARTIER
STATE PARK**
Route 12
Morristown
(315) 375-6371
Open mid-May through Columbus Day
Amenities: boat launches, boat rentals, campsites, dockage, dumping stations, food, grills, nature trails, pavilions, picnic tables, playgrounds, powerboats, showers, swimming beach, tent/trailer sites
Activities: fishing, hunting

**KEEWAYDIN
STATE PARK**
46165 NYS Route 12
Alexandria Bay
(315) 482-3331
Open Memorial Day until Labor Day
Amenities: boat launches, campsites, dockage, grills, marina, pump stations, playgrounds, picnic tables, powerboats, showers, swimming pool, tent/trailer sites
Activities: fishing, ice fishing

**KRING POINT
STATE PARK**
25950 Kring Point Road
Redwood
(315) 482-2444
Open from last Friday in April until Columbus Day
Amenities: boat launches, cabins, campsites, dockage, dumping stations, grills, pavilions, picnic tables, playgrounds, powerboats, showers, swimming beach, tent/trailer sites
Activities: fishing, hunting

**LONG POINT
STATE PARK**
7495 State Park Road
Three Mile Bay
(315) 649-5258
Open early May to Columbus Day
Amenities: boat launches, campsites, dockage, dumping stations, laundromat, pavilions, picnic tables, playgrounds, powerboats, showers, tent/trailer sites
Activities: fishing, hunting

**MACOMB RESERVATION
STATE PARK**
201 Campsite Road
Schuyler Falls
(518) 643-9952
Open mid-May to Labor Day
Amenities: boat rentals, camper recreation, campsites, dumping stations, grills, nature trails, pavilions, picnic tables, playgrounds, playing fields, showers, swimming beach, tent/trailer sites
Activities: fishing, hiking, recreation programs, snowmobiling, snowshoeing trails, X-country skiing

MARY ISLAND STATE PARK
Accessible only by water
(315) 482-2722
Open Memorial Day to Labor Day

Amenities: campsites, dockage, grills, picnic tables, showers
Activities: fishing

POINT AU ROCHE STATE PARK
19 Camp Red Cloud Road
Plattsburgh
(518) 563-0369
Open year-round

Amenities: boat launches, grills, nature trails, pavilions, picnic tables, playgrounds, playing fields, powerboats, showers, swimming beach

Activities: biking, fishing, hiking, ice fishing, recreation programs, snowshoeing trails, X-country skiing

ROBERT G. WEHLE STATE PARK
5182 State Park Road
Henderson
(315) 938-5302
Open year-round from sunrise to sunset

Amenities: cottages, picnic tables
Activities: biking, hiking, hunting, recreation programs, snowshoeing trails, tennis, X-country skiing

ROBERT MOSES STATE PARK
32 Beach Marina Road
Massena
(315) 769-8663
Open mid-May until mid-October

Amenities: boat launches, boat rentals, cabins, camper recreation, campsites, dockage, dumping stations, grills, marina, museum/visitor center, pavilions, picnic tables, playgrounds, playing fields, powerboats, showers, swimming beach, tent/trailer sites

Activities: biking, fishing, hunting, recreation programs, snowshoeing trails, X-country skiing

ROCK ISLAND LIGHTHOUSE STATE PARK
Accessible by boat only
Fisher's Landing
(315) 775-6886
Open mid-May until mid-September

Amenities: dockage, gift shop, museum/visitors center, scenic views

SACKETS HARBOR BATTLEFIELD STATE HISTORIC SITE
504 West Main Street
Sackets Harbor
(315) 646-4634

Amenities: guided and self-guided tours, exhibits, restored Navy Yard and Commandant's House

SOUTHWICK BEACH STATE PARK
8119 Southwicks Place
Henderson
(315) 846-5338
Open early-May through Columbus Day

Amenities: campsites, dumping stations, food, grills, nature trails, picnic tables, playgrounds, playing fields, showers, swimming beach, tent/trailer sites

Activities: fishing, hiking, hunting, snowshoeing trails, X-country skiing

WATERSON POINT STATE PARK
44927 Cross Island Road
Fineview
(315) 482-2722
Open Memorial Day to Labor Day

Amenities: dockage, pavilions, picnic tables, powerboats

Activities: fishing

WELLESLEY ISLAND STATE PARK
44927 Cross Island Road
Fineview
(315) 482-2722
Open year-round

Amenities: Boat launches, boat rentals, cabins, camper recreation, campsites, cottages, dockage, dumping stations, food, grills, interpretive signs, marina, museum/visitors center, nature trails, pavilions, picnic tables, playgrounds, playing fields, power boats, scenic views, showers, swimming beach, tent/trailer sites

Activities: biking, fishing, golf, hiking, hunting, ice fishing, snowshoeing trails, X-country skiing

WESTCOTT BEACH STATE PARK
Route 3
Henderson
(315) 646-2239
Open early-May through Columbus Day

Amenities: boat launches, camper reception, campsites, dockage, dumping stations, food, grills, pavilions, picnic tables, playgrounds, playing fields, powerboats, showers, swimming beach, tent/trailer sites

Activities: fishing, hiking, hunting, recreation programs, snowshoeing trails, X-country skiing

WHETSTONE GULF STATE PARK
6065 West Road
Lowville
(315) 376-6630
Open mid-May until September

Amenities: campsites, dumping stations, grills, nature trails, pavilions, picnic tables, playgrounds, showers, swimming beach, tent/trailer sites

Activities: fishing, hiking, hunting, snowmobiling, snowshoeing trails, X-country skiing

Stock Car Races

ADAMS CENTER RACETRACK, Adams Center

ADIRONDACK INTERNATIONAL SPEEDWAY
8512 Artz Road, Castorland, (315) 346-6624
www.adirondackspeedway.com
Car racing track in Lewis County, NY. The track 0.5-mile oval with superior asphalt. The facility includes a campground complete with bathrooms and showers, picnic areas and large pavilion.

CAN-AM SPEEDWAY
21047 NY-411, La Fargeville, (315) 658-4431   www.racecanam.com
Cam-Am Speedway of a ½ mile dirt oval raceway located in La Fargeville, Town of Orleans, NY. Located just a few miles from the Thousand Islands on New York State Route 411. It draws competitors and fans from both sides of the Canada-United States border.

CORNWALL MOTOR SPEEDWAY
16981 Cornwall Centre Road, Long Sault, On KOC 1 PO, Canada
(613)-938-3945, www.cornwallspeedway.com
The Cornwall Motor Speedway is a ¼ mile dirt track near the community of Cornwall, Ontario, Canada. The track opened in 1970 and runs weekly racing on Sunday evenings. Weekly race classes include modified sportsman, pro stock, semi pro and mini stock.

BROCKVILLE ONTARIO SPEEDWAY
Temperance Lake Road, Brockville, ON K6V 5T4, Canada
(613) 345-6324, www.brockvillespeedway.com
The Brockville Ontario Speedway is a 3/8-mile dirt track in the city of Brockville, Ontario, Canada. Commonly known as "The BOS," the track has been running a weekly racing schedule for most summers since 1969.

EVANS MILLS RACEWAY PARK
28412 Steinhilber Road, Evans Mills
(315) 658-8019, www.evansmillsracewaypark.com
The Evans Mills Raceway Park has a race every Saturday night at 6:30 p.m. The divisions they have are: Sportsman Modifieds; Pro Late Models; INEX Legends; Sports Compact/Thunder Stock; 6-Cylinder Stringers; and have added a Prolate Model Class.

MOHAWK INTERNATIONAL RACEWAY – "FROGTOWN RACETRACK"
Akwesasne Reservation, Hogansburg
(518) 358-9017, www.mohawkintlraceway.com
The Mohawk International Raceway has 6-divisions adding new Super Stock Cars. They feature live entertainment on Saturdays and have food available for patrons. Open on Friday and Saturday.

PLATTSBURGH AIRBORNE SPEEDWAY
70 Broderick Road, Plattsburgh
(518) 561-0654, www.plattsburghairbornespeedway.com
Longtime destination for car races and truck events on a half-mile semi-banked asphalt oval.

Swimming Pools

OGDENSBURG MUNICIPAL POOL
100 Washington St
Ogdensburg
(315) 393-0133

WILLIAM J. FLYNN MUNICIPAL SWIMMING POOL
833 Woodbury St
Watertown

FAIRGROUNDS PUBLIC SWIMMING POOL
825 Earl St
Watertown

THOMPSON PARK SPLASH PAD
Thompson Park
Watertown

The splash pad in Watertown's Thompson Park is fun for kids of all ages on a hot day. It features equipment for older and younger kids and is handicap accessible. Thompson Park has a zoo as well as a monument to soldiers of the 10th Mountain Division.

Train Trips

ADIRONDACK SCENIC RAILROAD
19 Depot St., Saranac Lake Union Station. (518) 891-3238. Averyville Rd., Lake Placid Station. General Information: (315) 724-0700 or 877-508-6728. May-October. www.adirondackrr.com
Historic train stations at Saranac Lake (1904) and Lake Placid (1903) are the departure points from the 20 mile scenic round-trip excursions that run between Saranac Lake and Lake Placid. Spring, summer and fall foliage rides. Tuesday through Sunday. Depart Lake Placid Station 10 a.m., 12:30 p.m. and 3 p.m. Depart Saranac Lake Station 11:15 a.m., 1:45 p.m. and 4:15 p.m.

POLAR EXPRESS
Live the magic of the classic polar express train ride story with the Adirondack Scenic Railroad. Depart from Utica Union Station and travel while being served hot chocolate and cookies. When you arrive at the North Pole, Santa will board the train visiting with each family and giving each child their first gift of Christmas in the form of a Silver Bell, just like in the book or movie. Children (and parents) are encouraged to come in pajamas. Don't forget your cameras, you'll want to capture the memories and your time with Santa.

Options: First Class Ride. For a first class ride, travel to the North Pole in a Cocoa Class Car. The hot chocolate chefs are the hosts for you in the first class car. Families are served cookies and hot chocolate in a Souvenir mug while seated at a table setting for four. Coach Class Ride. Train style seating with cookies and hot chocolate. Santa visits with each and every family during the return trip.
Start times: Daily 4 pm and 6:30 pm and Wed additional 4:30 pm trip.
Duration: 2 hours
Cost: Coach Class: Adults $46
 Children $38
 First Class: Adults $67.50
  Children $57.50

SKI TRAIN North Creek, NY
The Ski Train to North Creek, which had not operated since the 1940s. Was revived in 2011 under the Saratoga and North Creek Railroad. The new train runs from the Saratoga Springs Amtrak Station to the North Creek Depot, with a free shuttle for that point to Gore Mountain. Breakfast and lunch are served on the trains. On Saturdays, the peak point of operation, there are two north bound and three south bound trips.

THENDARA TIMBER TRAIN
Thendara Station-
Otter Lake/Carter Station
Thendara is 1 mile south of Old Forge. 800-819-2291. summer: Wednesday through Sunday, 10 a.m., 12:30 p.m. and 2:45 p.m. Fall: Tuesday through Sunday, 10 a.m., 12:30 p.m. and 2:45 p.m. Departures form the Thendara Station.

WILDERNESS ADVENTURE
Union Station, Utica, NY - Thendara Station/Old Forge.
Summer: Tuesday. Fall, Thursday through Saturday. Shuttle to Old Forge during layover. Depart Union Station 9:30 a.m. Arrive Thendara 11:45 a.m.; Depart Thendara Station 4:30 p.m. Arrive Union Station 6:30 p.m.

ADIRONDACK GATEWAY
Union Station, Utica, NU-Kayuta Trestle/Forestport. Summer: Tuesday. Fall: Monday and Tuesday. Depart Union Station 9:30 a.m. Return to Union Station 1p.m.

OLD FORGE
Take an Adirondack adventure and observe pristine woods and wildlife. Many specials during the week including train robberies, eco-tours, murder mysteries, dinner and party train and barbecues. Spectacular fall foliage trips. Runs May - October. Call for free brochure of schedules, toll free, 1-877-508-6728.
www.adirondackrr.com

100 Waterfalls

Among the greatest natural attractions of the North Country are its majestic waterfalls. No matter what the season, you can enjoy the falls where for over 200 years, area residents have built their homes and mills. They also have been drawn to them for recreation and relaxation. Whether you swim, fish, canoe, kayak, take photographs or hike near the waterfalls, it is a trip to be remembered.

Photos, descriptions and directions can be found to the following at **www.visitstlc.com**. A printed Waterfalls Guide is also available from the St. Lawrence County Chamber of Commerce.

- Allen Falls, Parishville
- Cascade Falls, Canton
- Greenwood Falls, Harrisville
- Harper Falls, Russell
- High Falls, Wanakena
- Jamestown Falls, Sevey Corners
- Lampson Falls, Clare
- Little River Falls, Canton
- Moody Falls, Colton
- Olmstead Pond Loop, Wanakena
- Plum Brook Falls, Russell
- Rushton Falls, Canton
- Stone Valley, Colton

Other References:
Northern New York Waterfalls **www.nnywaterfalls.com** Directions, descriptions and photos to waterfalls in 16 northern New York counties. Listings are alphabetical, by county and by river.

Family-Friendly Waterfall Hikes in the Adirondacks, by John Haywood, is a compilation of easy and shorter waterfall hikes from across the Adirondacks.

TOOLEY POND ROAD INCLUDES A 16-MILE SECTION OF THE SOUTH BRANCH OF THE GRASSE RIVER. ALONG THIS STRETCH SEVEN MAJOR WATERFALLS EXIST: RAINBOW FALLS, BULKHEAD FALLS, FLAT ROCK FALLS, TWIN FALLS, SINCLAIR FALLS, BASFORD FALLS AND COPPER ROCK FALLS. THEIR CHARACTERISTICS RANGE FROM THE 55-FOOT DROP OF TWIN FALLS TO THE GENTLE SLOPES OF SINCLAIR FALLS, A PERFECT PLACE TO PICNIC.

CASCADE FALLS AND RUSHTON FALLS
located in the Grasse River in Canton can be seen from a hiking trail. Visit the Willow Island Park located at 2 Main Street in Canton to access the trail. Park trails may not be open in the winter.

Wildlife Refuges

AUSABLE MARSH STATE WILDLIFE MANAGEMENT AREA
Route 9, Peru
A fertile delta at the mouth of the Ausable River managed by the state DEC for a variety of recreational and scientific purposes including: natural resources education, wildlife observation, photography, fishing, trapping, hunting, and canoeing

CHAZY HIGHLANDS WILDLIFE MANAGEMENT AREA
(Department of Environmental Conservation)
Town of Dannemora, Clinton County
Contact: Region 5 Wildlife
PO Box 296, Ray Brook
(518) 897-1219
The primary purposes are for wildlife management, wildlife habitat management and wildlife-dependent recreation. Offers hunting, trapping and fishing.

COLLINS LANDING WILDLIFE MANAGEMENT AREA
Collins Landing Road, Orleans
Open year-round
Contact: Bureau of Wildlife
317 Washington St
Watertown
(315) 785-2263

OTTER CREEK PRESERVE AND NATURE TRAIL
Alexandria Bay
(315) 686-5345
Open year-round
Offers 1.9 miles of trails for walking, hiking, X-country skiing and snowshoeing

Zoos

AQUA ZOO
43681 NYS Route 12, Alexandria Bay
(315) 482-5771
Open Wednesday through Sunday
11:00am – 6:00pm (12:00 Sunday)
Off Season hours Wednesday through Saturday 4:00pm – 9:00 pm
www.aquazoo.com
One of the largest privately owned aquariums of its kind in the United States or Canada. Hundreds of varieties of marine life on display and nearly 20,000 gallons of fresh and sea water.

NEW YORK STATE ZOO AT THOMPSON PARK
1 Thompson Park, Watertown
(315) 782-6180
www.nyszoo.org
Open year-round (Weekends only November to March)
Spanning 32 acres, the zoo is home to a variety of species native to New York State featuring a pond, butterfly house and trail system. It is the only zoo in the world to exhibit species native to New York State. Thompson Park also has a playground, picnic area, pool and splash park.

OLD MCDONALD'S FARM
14369 County Road 145, Sackets Harbor
(315) 583-5737
www.oldmcdonaldhasafarm.com
Open May through October
An educational, agricultural, hands-on adventure for kids of all ages with over 1000 farm animals, a Wizard of Oz themed hay ride, miniature golf, bounce houses, pumpkin patch, corn maze, dairy farm tours, pony rides, gift shop, produce stand, café and ice cream stand.

Just Over The Border

Ontario, Canada

There is so much to explore a short drive away in southern Ontario. Remember to bring proper IDs and any other necessary documents to be able to cross the border. Learn more at:
www.ezbordercrossing.com
www.cbsa-asfc.gc.ca

UPPER CANADA VILLAGE
13740 County Road 2, Morrisburg, Ontario 800-437-2233 or (613) 543-4328
www.uppercanadavillage.com
At this living history museum, step back in time to explore over 40 authentic historic buildings in an 1860s riverside setting; learn from "19th Century" inhabitants; travel along a canal in a horse-drawn Tow Scow; take a ride on the Carry-All wagon along village streets or ride the miniature train; dine at a heritage restaurant and shop at the Village Store. There are many children's educational programs and activities (including summer camps), a few special-event festivals, and guided tours are available. Don't miss their Alight At Night outdoor light festival in December, with close to one million lights adorning the historic buildings and trees (alightatnight.ca). Admission fees apply. Free for children 4 and under.

PREHISTORIC WORLD
5446 Upper Canada Road, Morrisburg, Ontario (613) 543-2503
facebook.com/pages/Prehistoric-World/582066475303908
Ontario's own Jurassic Park! Stroll along nature trials and discover full size replicas of relics from the past. Over 50 life-size reproductions of prehistoric animals displayed in a realistic natural setting. Open daily 10am-4pm, May 24-September 1. Admission fees apply.

FORT WELLINGTON NATIONAL HISTORIC SITE OF CANADA
370 Vankoughnet Street, Prescott, Ontario (613) 925-2896,
www.pc.gc.ca/en/lhn-nhs/on/wellington
Visit the largest blockhouse in Canada. Built to protect against American attack in the War of 1812 and expanded near the Rebellions of 1837-1838. Explore the original fortifications and an 1812-era gunboat, try on a costume, take part in a military drill, witness a cannon firing, taste period treats cooked over an open fire, or play games from long ago. There is also a waterfront walking trail. Children can get the most out of their visit by participating in the Fort Wellington Xplorers Program. Xplorers booklets are available at the Visitor Centre and offer fun activities that guide discovery. Kids receive a certificate and a souvenir when they turn in a completed booklet. Open Mid-May through early October. Admission fees under $4. Free for youth aged 17 and under.

BATTLE OF THE WINDMILL NATIONAL HISTORIC SITE OF CANADA
County Road 2 East, Prescott, Ontario (613) 925-1838
www.pc.gc.ca/en/lhn-nhs/on/windmill Climb into an 1830s

stone windmill built on the north shore of the St. Lawrence River just east of Prescott. The site was the scene of an 1838 battle between 200 Americans sympathetic to political reform in Canada and local Canadian militia and British soldiers. Audio-visual presentation available and exhibits on view. Open summer months only. Admission fee $2. Free for youth aged 17 and under.

BROCKVILLE MUSEUM
5 Henry Street, Brockville, Ontario
(613) 342- 4397
www.brockvillemuseum.com
A visit to the Brockville Museum offers a glimpse into the social and industrial history of Ontario's first incorporated town. Through a variety of thematic and interpretive displays, the museum shares the stories of the people who have shaped this riverfront community for over 200 years. The museum offers children's Discovery Packs filled with engaging exhibit-based activities - a great way for kids to explore and learn. Tours are available in English and French. Bonus: Take a walk through the nearby Historic Railway Tunnel just down the road at 8 Brock Street. Built between 1854-1860, it is the oldest railway tunnel in Canada and runs under the downtown core of the city for 4 blocks www.brockvillerailwaytunnel.com
Open Spring through Fall only. Admission by donation.

BROCKVILLE AQUATARIUM AT TALL SHIPS LANDING
6 Broad Street, Brockville, Ontario
(613) 342-6789
www.aquatarium.ca
A 33,000+ square foot climate-controlled aquarium and discovery centre that offers a full range of activities for kids, teens, and adults. Guests can participate in hands-on interactive exhibits as well as see and learn about the many species of fish and animals, such as otters, native to the St. Lawrence River.

"Science Saturdays" program for children aged 6-12, a 2 hour session of exciting experiments and creative crafts and summer camp sessions offered. Admission fees apply.

Free for children 3 and under.

FULFORD PLACE
287 King Street East, Brockville, Ontario
(613) 498-3003
www.heritagetrust.on.ca/en/properties/fulford-place
A National Historic Site owned and operated by the Ontario Heritage Foundation. Built between 1899-1901, this 35 room Edwardian mansion, designed by New York architect Albert W. Fuller and filled with original furnishings, evokes the opulent lifestyle of Canada's industrial elite at the turn of the last century. Learn about the Fulfords and how the local family business, G.T. Fulford and Co., made them millionaires through the innovative global marketing of "Dr. William's Pink Pills for Pale People". Wander the beautifully restored Olmstead Italianate Gardens. Tours available.
Open seasonally, call for details.
Admission fee $6. Free for children 6 and under.

FORT HENRY
1 Fort Henry Drive, Kingston, Ontario
800-437-2233
www.forthenry.com
Built from 1832 to 1837 this Fort protected the naval dockyard at Point Frederick, the entrance of the Rideau Canal and town of Kingston. Once inside the wooden gates of this historic site and museum, visitors enter the realm of 19th century military and civilian life, experience guided tours, scenic views, and precision military demonstrations. Children can attend a replica Victorian School to practice writing a letter home and enjoy a storytelling session. There's even a Ghosts of Fort Henry Walking Tour for those brave enough to attend! Admission fees apply. Free for children 4 and under.

SKYWOOD ECO ADVENTURE PARK
1278 Thousand Islands Parkway, Mallory, Ontario   (613) 923-5120
www.skywoodzip.com
Canada's largest aerial adventure park offers a series of guided and self-led zip line courses that are 2-3 hours long. Hike through a series of unique games including bridges, swings, nets, and zip lines as you go from one treetop platform to the

next. The park offers a Children's Discovery Course for kids aged 5-12, as well as an accessible zip line. The Treewalk Village explores seven different treehouses connected by log bridges and ramps, slides, and zip lines that children as young as 3 years are welcome to explore. Reservations are required. Prices vary depending on length of time and age.

GLENGARRY HIGHLAND GAMES
34 Fair Street, Maxville, Ontario
888-298-1666
www.glengarryhighlandgames.com
For three days each August (since 1948!) this small farming community hosts a variety of traditional Scottish sporting competitions and cultural events. Don't miss the outstanding display of music, dance, sports, fiddling, pageantry, and tradition! Over 50 pipe bands are put through their paces, more than 200 dancers defy gravity at the Highland Dance Competition, and giants hurl telephone-sized cabers and 50-pound iron hammers in the Heavyweight Competition. There is also a Children's Mini Games and a Wee Bairns Tent with a petting zoo, face painting, puppet show, and music. Enjoy Scottish food and browse the many vendors offering Celtic jewelry, giftware, ironworks, and clothing. This is an incredible and memorable event. Admission fees apply. Free for children 12 and under.

Explore these tourism pages for more to do:

Brockville Tourism:
www.brockvilletourism.com

Kingston Tourism:
www.visitkingston.ca

Prescott Tourism:
www.prescott.ca/en/index.asp

Ontario Tourism:
www.ontariotravel.net/en/home

South Eastern Ontario Tourism:
www.southeasternontario.ca

Cornwall

This small city is really just a step over the border and has a lot to offer. Explore the tourism website for dates of festival events, concert series, or the many places to eat. You can also stop in at the tourism office located in the Civic Center in Lameroux Park for printed city maps and talk to their friendly staff about where to go and what to do.

Cornwall Tourism:
www.cornwalltourism.com

LAMEROUX PARK
West Street, Cornwall, Ontario
The first right hand turn after crossing the border if you drive via Massena. Situated on the banks of the St. Lawrence River, there is more than meets the eye to explore in this park. There are huge grassy fields to play in, many picnic tables to lunch at, a playground and fabulous water play splash pad, and a bandshell where you can catch free concerts and movies in the summer months.

WATERFRONT TRAIL
www.cornwalltourism.com/measure-your-way-along-the-waterfront-trail/
Walk, bike, scooter, or stroll along the portion of the Great Lakes Waterfront Trail that runs through the park along the St. Lawrence River. Free parking and nearby bike rentals available.

CORNWALL COMMUNITY MUSEUM AND ARCHIVES
www.cornwallcommunitymuseum.wordpress.com A restored 1840 Loyalist home that features archival materials, periodic displays of historic furniture, textiles, and household items. Free.

HISTORIC SDG JAIL
www.historicsdgjail.com
Located just across the street from the park, this County Jail building was constructed in 1833 and remained operational over a period of 168 years. The facility housed inmates from Cornwall and neighboring counties. Men, women, and children of all ages were incarcer-

ated here for various types of offenses including being in debt and committing murder. It is considered one of the oldest public structures in Ontario. Historical artifacts and displays are arranged around the building. Guided tours are available during the summer months. Admission fees apply. Free for children 4 and under.

CORNWALL CIVIC COMPLEX
The heart of the complex is the Ed Lumley Arena, a modern ice rink that hosts a variety of hockey championships and professional ice skating events, and the Aultsville Theater www.aultsvilletheatre.com, which offers a rich variety of music concerts, theater, and other performances. The complex also includes:
Aquatic Centre - (613) 933-3586
www.cornwall.ca/AquaticCentre
The centre features a world class 6-lane, 25 metre pool along with a two-story water slide, toddler leisure pool, and spacious whirlpool. Open year-round, Monday-Sunday 6am-8pm. Over 40 public swimming opportunities per week. Check website for fees and more details.
Sports Hall of Fame - is located in the Civic Center, and includes memorabilia and photos of over 300 notable athletes.

CURLING CENTRE
www.cornwallcurling.ca. This facility is home to over 500 curlers and hosts a variety of bonspiels throughout the year that are open to public attendance.

CORNWALL HISTORIC WALKING TOUR
This tour begins in Lamoureux Park. It features three separate walks through the waterfront, downtown, and the Le Village area that can be enjoyed together or individually. There are 30 colorfully illustrated plaques along the way detailing historic scenes from Cornwall's past that together weave together the city's roots. You can follow the map: www.cornwalltourism.com/wp-content/uploads/2017/07/Cornwall-Historic-Walking-Tour-Map-1.pdf

ST. LAWRENCE POWER DEVELOPMENT SAUNDERS HYDRO DAM VISITOR CENTRE 2500B Second Street West, Cornwall, Ontario (613) 932-4563
www.opg.com/build-ing-strong-and-safe-communities/our-communities/eastern-ontario/saunders-visitor-centre
Showcases the history of the St. Lawrence Seaway and Power Project, the communities and people affected, and great biodiversity stories like the American eel. Offers exciting and informative interactive displays and summer kid's programs. Closes for the season in October. Free.

PUBLIC SKATING
www.cornwall.ca/skating
Check out indoor ice skating at the Benson Centre, 800 7th Avenue (613) 938-9898, or have fun at one of the many outdoor rinks

SEAWAY VALLEY THEATRE COMPANY
www.svtc.ca This not-for-profit, non-commercial theatre company stages four plays each year: a Broadway style musical, a musical play for children, and two comedies with cabaret-style seating. The 2019 season offered Mary Poppins, Mamma Mia, and Nunsense. Venues include the Aultsville Theater at the Cornwall Civic Centre and sometimes local schools. Check website for current shows.

A Little Bit Further . . . .

Ottawa

The capital of Canada, Ottawa is a great city to explore and a short distance from St. Lawrence County. Located in the southeastern part of Ontario, it overlooks the Ottawa River, and the Rideau River and Canal flow through it. One of winter's delights is to ice skate the full length of that canal, especially during the Winterlude festival. The Canadian Parliament buildings are located on Parliament Hill along with the Supreme Court and National library. The city is home to over 25 museums, including seven national museums. From Canadian history, to priceless world-class art, to the heroic tales of those who fought bravely for Canada, to enormous dinosaur fossils and to the World's largest indoor collection of totem poles, Ottawa's many museums have something to offer everyone, no matter what your interests might be. The city also hosts dozens of festivals appealing to just about every interest and across the entire calendar. We've included a sampling of highlights here, but be sure to check out the tourism pages listed below for much more!

Ottawa Tourism: **www.ottawatourism.ca**

Ottawa Festivals: **www.ottawafestivals.ca**

CANADA CHILDREN'S MUSEUM
100 Laurier Street, Gatineau, Quebec
819-776-8294
www.historymuseum.ca
Housed inside the Canadian Museum of History, just across the Ottawa River from downtown. The museum lets kids travel around the world engaging in hands-on interactive displays. Visit an Egyptian pyramid, clamber aboard a lavishly decorated Pakistani bus and a three-wheeled auto rickshaw from Thailand, step inside a Bedouin tent and homes from India or Mexico. Start your visit by obtaining a Children's Museum passport and collect stamps along the way. Access included with admission fees to the Canadian Museum of History.

CANADIAN MUSEUM OF HISTORY
100 Laurier Street, Gatineau, Ontario
800-555-5621
www.historymuseum.ca
Canada's largest and most popular cultural institution. Located on a spectacular riverfront site, just across the Ottawa River from downtown, the Museum offers an unparalleled view of Ottawa's historic skyline. Permanent exhibitions include the majestic Grand Hall, housing the world's largest indoor collection of totem poles; the First Peoples Hall, dedicated to the history and achievements of Canada's Indigenous Peoples; and the highly popular Canada Hall, which takes visitors on a cross-Canada journey through 1,000 years of history. Other favorite features include the Canadian Children's Museum, the Canadian Postal Museum, and the IMAX® Theatre. The Panorama Café, Bistro Boreal, and Second Cup coffee offer a variety of food options while visiting. Admission fees apply. Free for children 2 and under.

CANADA SCIENCE AND TECHNOLOGY MUSEUM
1867 St. Laurent Boulevard,
Ottawa, Ontario
866-442-4416
www.ingeniumcanada.org
This museum is devoted to the history, principles, and applications of science and technology. It has loads of hands-on and digital exhibits and displays covering energy, communications, computers, and land, marine, and space travel.

Exhibitions include a large display of steam locomotives, cars, and domestic appliances over the years, as well as the Crazy Kitchen, the ZOOM Children's Innovation Zone, Artifact Alley, and the Exploratek maker studio. There's a cafeteria on site. Admission fees apply. Free for children 2 and under.

CANADIAN AVIATION AND SPACE MUSEUM
11 Aviation Parkway,
Ottawa, Ontario
800-463-2038
www.ingeniumcanada.org
This museum is home to Canada's top aeronautical exhibits, and among the best in the world, with a collection of 120 aircraft from the early 1900s, warplanes from both World Wars, jets, and bush planes. Admission fees apply. Free for children 2 and under.

CANADIAN AGRICULTURE AND FOOD MUSEUM
901 Prince of Wales Drive
Ottawa, Ontario
www.ingeniumcanada.org
Located at Ottawa's Central Experimental Farm, this 'museum' is a working farm in the heart of the city and offers programs and exhibitions on Canada's agricultural heritage and food literacy.

Visit the animal barns and explore exhibits including Tractors, Food Preservation, and the Discovery Park. Programming includes special weekend theme events, summer day campus, and interpretive tours.
Admission fees apply.

Free for children 2 and under.
CANADIAN MUSEUM OF NATURE
240 Mcleod Street, Ottawa, Ontario
800-263-4433
www.nature.ca
This museum houses many treasures of Canada's natural history, including one of the biggest collections of taxidermy animals and birds in a variety of natural-setting dioramas, live animals, mounted insects, and dinosaur fossils. There's even an enormous blue whale skeleton! The Nature Café offers snacks and light dishes. Admission fees apply. Free for children 2 and under.

CANADIAN WAR MUSEUM
1 Vimy Place
Ottawa, Ontario
800-555-5621
www.warmuseum.ca
This museum showcases Canada's rich military history through artifacts, personal stories, artwork, photos, and interactive presentations. Tour the extensive exhibitions in this building renowned for its symbolic architecture and expand your knowledge of the conflicts that shaped Canada - from the colonial days in the 1600s, the War of 1812, World War I, World War II and more recent peacekeeping missions. Displays include military aircraft, tanks and vehicles.
Café on site. Admission fees apply.

Free for children 2 and under.
BYTOWN MUSEUM
1 Canal Lane, Ottawa, Ontario
(613) 234-4570
www.bytownmuseum.com
Beside the entrance to the locks to the Rideau Canal and steps away from the Chateau Laurier Hotel stands the Commissariat, the oldest stone building in Ottawa and the home of the Bytown Museum. This museum explores Ottawa's history from the early years of Rideau Canal construction, through the days of 'rough-and-tumble' Bytown, to its emergence as Canada's capital. Activities include a postcard scavenger hunt. A six-language audio guide available. Open year round. Admission fees apply. *Read about pedestrian access to the museum on their web page.

BANK OF CANADA MUSEUM
30 Bank Street,
Ottawa, Ontario
(613) 782-8914
www.bankofcanadamuseum.ca
Enter the heart of the economic system and explore fun, hands-on, interactive exhibits that cover everything from how people's expectations affect the health of an economy to how inflation targeting works (hint: you get to fly a rocket ship!). Mixed in with all the high-tech interactives are informative videos, multimedia

stations and old-school exhibits featuring centuries' worth of economic artifacts: from shells once used as money, to bank notes made from tree bark, together with their history and lore. The museum offers the most complete collection of Canadian bank notes, coins and tokens in the world. You can learn about the history of currency in Canada and how bank notes are designed and printed today. Free Admission.

NATIONAL GALLERY OF CANADA
380 Sussex Drive
Ottawa, Ontario
800-319-2787
www.gallery.ca
This modern glass-encased building uses dramatic natural lighting to showcase Canada's and the art world's great treasures. Over 1200 works in the permanent collection are on view. The museum's construction includes the historic Rideau Chapel, along with its collection of sacredart and silver pieces. Of special interest are the Indigenous Galleries, the Canadian Photography Institute, collections of Old Masters, and works by members of the Group of Seven. Admission fees apply. A cafeteria, the 7 Tapas Bar, and Second Cup coffee offer a variety of food options while visiting. Admission fees apply. Free for children 11 and under.

You might also want to check out:

CHANGING OF THE GUARD AT PARLIAMENT HILL
111 Wellington Street
Ottawa, Ontario
www.ottawatourism.ca
This parade is a colorful spectacle of pomp, pageantry and music that takes place on the front lawn of Parliament Hill every morning from late June through late August. The Ceremonial Guard is drawn from two regiments - the Governor General's Foot Guards and the Canadian Grenadier Guards. They are accompanied by their own Regimental Band and Pipers who provide musical support for the ceremony. The Ceremonial Guardsmen taking part are mostly university and college students who are reservists in the Canadian Forces. Arrive on the lawn of Parliament Hill at 9:45am to obtain a good viewing spot and hear the audio presentation which explains the symbolism and history of the ceremony. Free.

ALTITUDE CLIMBING GYM
35 Saint-Raymond Boulevard
Gatineau, Quebec
(819) 205-0959
www.altitudegym.ca
Offers a unique indoor rock-climbing gym experience with more than 100 routes up to 45 feet high and many bouldering areas. Beginners and experts can practice climbing in all its forms. Try the Clip 'N Climb theme park, a stunning action packed activity with 34 individually themed climbing challenges that provide healthy challenging fun for the whole family! Located across the river from downtown Ottawa. Equipment and gear available for rental. Daily rates or memberships available.

FUNHAVEN
1050 Baxter Road
Ottawa, Ontario
(613) 828-4386
www.funhaven.com
The name says it all for this large, indoor, fun play space. Activities include a laser tag arena, a giant jungle gym, high-tech mini bowling lanes, video and arcade games, bumper cars, a rock wall to climb, and escape room experiences. There's a café on site with fresh-baked pizza and a make-your-own sundae bar. This is a great cold-weather or rainy day place to expend some energy! A tiered pricing model offers choice, depending on what you want to do there and how long you want to stay and play.

A Few Festivals

Check the Ottawa tourism site for more events and exact dates.
www.ottawatourism.ca

WINTERLUDE
www.canada.ca
Held annually over the first three weekends in February, the focal point of this winter celebration is the 5 miles of the

Rideau Canal Skateway where thousands of skaters of all levels can be found gliding, riding in sleighs for rent, or stopping at one of the many food vendors set up on the ice for a snack, a hot drink and a rest by a warm outdoor fire. Jacques-Cartier Park is transformed into a giant snow playground, complete with ice slides and snow sculptures and Confederation Park becomes a crystal garden of glittering ice sculptures! Free.

TULIP FESTIVAL
www.tulipfestival.ca
The Canadian Tulip Festival takes place in and around Ottawa every spring (usually May), displaying over a million tulips in over 100 varieties.

The festival's origins lie in Canada's role in both liberating the Netherlands and hosting members of the Dutch royal family during the Second World War. After the war, the Netherlands began gifting Canada with tulip bulbs in gratitude, a tradition that continues to this day.

The inaugural festival was held in 1953. The largest display is found in Commissioners Park (corner of Preston Street and the Queen Elizabeth Driveway), on the shores of Dow's Lake, as well as along the canal. Don't miss this beautiful explosion of color! Free.

BLUESFEST
www.ottawbluesfest.ca
One of the largest international music events, with over 200 varied music acts on several outdoor stages (hint: there's something for everyone, it's not just the Blues!). Held annually over a couple weeks in July at the LeBreton Flats. Single or multi day passes available for purchase.

OTTAWA CHILDREN'S FESTIVAL
www.ottawachildrensfestival.ca
This is a five day extravaganza of theatre, dance, and music that focuses on enriching school curriculum and promoting the arts as an integral part of children's education. Usually held in early May.

The festival offers performances and interactive activities appropriate for children of ALL ages! Their motto: Be Inspired, Be Creative, Express Yourself! Some activities are free but admission prices apply for many performances.

DRAGON BOAT FESTIVALS
www.dragonboat.net
www.icedragonboat.ca
Two festivals, one in water, one on ice, showcase large-scale canoe-style boats elaborately decorated with Chinese dragon heads and tails, paddled by teams of up to 50 rowers, accompanied by a drummer who beats out their sprinting rhythm (it's quite a sight!) The festivals include free concerts, local cuisine, multi-cultural performances and a variety of family activities. The Tim Hortons Dragon Boat Festival is held annually for four days in June in Mooney's Bay where the Rideau River and Rideau Canal split. The BeaverTails Ice Dragon Boat Festival is held in early February on the Rideau Canal Skateway. Over 200 athlete teams from all over the world join to compete in these races. This is heart-racing fun even as a spectator! Free.

Sharon Vegh Williams
Executive Director, NCCM

Sharon Vegh Williams, PhD, has worked in museums and schools for 30 years. She is the Co-Founder and Executive Director of the North Country Children's Museum. Sharon was awarded the Provost Fellowship at the University of Rochester where she completed her doctorate in multicultural education. Her writing has been published in the Association of Children's Museums Quarterly Journal, the Journal of American Indian Education, and Teacher Education Quarterly. Her book entitled Native Cultural Competency in Mainstream Schooling was published by Palgrave Macmillan. Sharon continues to research and write about museums.

At the North Country Children's Museum, learning is a hands-on, minds-on, interactive experience. With exhibits and daily programs that celebrate the cultural and geographical resources of the North Country, you'll find play areas and tinker spaces for all ages to get kids thinking, making, and doing. Build and balance in the Construction Zone or run the store in the Kids Co-Op and Bakery. Explore the Raquette River in the Adirondack Water Play exhibit or light up your mind with the STEAM Power everbright art wall. The Playspace, especially designed for crawlers, toddlers, and preschoolers, gets little ones moving with sensory and imaginative play. The North Country Children's Museum, where kids play to learn and grown-ups learn to play!

NORTH COUNTRY CHILDREN'S MUSEUM

About the Author

Dr. Kendall Taylor is a cultural historian who writes about people within the framework of social history. She has written two books about F. Scott and Zelda Fitzgerald: Sometimes Madness Is Wisdom, published by Random House/Ballantine which was nominated for a Pulitzer, and her most recent: The Gatsby Affair; Scott, Zelda and the Betrayal that Shaped An American Classic. Her study of the American artist, Philip Evergood: Never Separate From The Heart, is considered seminal in its field. Besides teaching at George Washington University, The American University and State University of New York, she also served as Head of the National Exhibitions Program at the Library of Congress, Academic Director of AU's Washington Semester Program in Art and Architecture, and Vice President for Planning and Research at Quaker Friends World College.

About the Designer

Sheila Rae Neal is a graphic designer and illustrator who is an Assistant professor at SUNY Potsdam. In addition to teaching as an adjunct for Pratt in Utica, she has taught at Mohawk Valley Community College, and SUNY Polytechnic. She is currently a Ph.D. candidate at the Institute for Doctoral Studies in the Visual Arts. While staff artist for the Press and Sun Bulletin, she designed their weekly entertainment section and published a full page illustration entitled "Seven Principles of Discipline" which was picked up by USA Today. She designed Nancy Gill's "Parents' Guide to School Selection in San Mateo/Santa Clara County" published by Haskala Press, and was Production Manager at Enjoy the City, Inc. where she designed over 100 books. She has exhibited art at the Windsor Whip Works Art Gallery, Delavan Art Gallery, and University of Hartford.

North Country Children's Museum
Membership

Become a member and enjoy yearlong, hands-on learning for you and your family. All members receive free admission, special discounts, and admission to weekend programs. All memberships are valid for 12 months. If your children are eligible for free or reduced lunch, see us about discounted membership rates. Purchase your membership online or in person at the front desk.

Family Membership: $85
Admits up to 2 adults and all children living in the same household .
Free admission to special weekend programs
10% discount on NCCM events, camps, classes, and birthday parties

Family Membership Plus: $115
Admits up to 2 adults and all children living in the same household, plus 2 additional adults.
Free admission to special weekend programs.
10% discount on NCCM events, camps, classes, and birthday parties

Giving Membership: $60
Donate a membership and give the gift of hands-on learning to a local family in need.

Discount Membership: $25
Annual family membership for those whose children qualify for free or reduced lunch. Register at front desk.

One Free Day Pass
to the
North Country Children's Museum

NORTH COUNTRY CHILDREN'S MUSEUM
northcountrychildrensmuseum.org

10 Raymond Street
Potsdam, NY 13676
(315) 274-9380

Valid during regular museum hours only on the day presented. Good for one single day pass for a single admission only. Limit one coupon per family or group per visit. All admittance policies, entrance rules, and restrictions apply. No discounts towards additional fees, services, or membership. Coupon must be presented at entry. Not valid during parties, specials, classes, or entrance into events which require additional fees. Not exchangeable for cash value. Non transferable. This coupon must be presented at entry and can not be reused or be refunded. Copies, prints, or duplications are not accepted. Redeemable only at the North Country Children's Museum, 10 Raymond Street, Potsdam, NY 13676. **Coupon expires 12-30-2023**

Editorial Committee

Standing (left to right):

Mary Cabral, Health Sciences Librarian, Clarkson University, Volunteer, NCCM, Hiking and X-Country enthusiast

Laurie Cappello, Former President, Potsdam Hospital Guild, Volunteer, NCCM

Pam Kemp Shepherd, Retired Speech-Language Pathologist, Volunteer, NCCM

Emily Skiff, Retired Social Worker, Volunteer, NCCM

Seated (left to right):

Kendall Taylor, Author

Kathleen Fitzgerald, Retired nurse and outdoor enthusiast, Volunteer, NCCM

Nancy Griffin, Member, Board of Trustees, NCCM, Retired Fundraiser, SUNY, Potsdam

Photo Credits:
John Ashley, Blue Fin Diving
Call of the Wild Sled Dog Tours
Laurie Cappello
Carol Hill Photography
Jonnie Claeys
Kathleen Fitzgerald
April Grant
Nancy Griffin
Sheila Rae Neal
Brooke Rouse
Pam Kemp Shepherd
St. Lawrence County Chamber of Commerce

This is the Second Edition of *Out and About* and we will be publishing revised versions in the future. If you discover something that should be added, have any suggestions or notice any errors, let our Museum front desk know, and happy day tripping!

A History of the
North Country Children's Museum

The North Country Children's Museum is a non-profit organization with a commitment to hands-on, minds-on learning. This mission is reflected in our permanent space in the Red Barn at 10 Raymond Street in historic Potsdam, NY, which opened doors to the public in summer 2018. The museum's exhibits celebrate the cultural and geographic resources of the North Country and provide opportunities for children and their families to play and learn together. In creating engaging, fun, and memorable educational experiences, NCCM provides space for children to try on the role of scientist, engineer and artist.

NCCM formed in 2012 by a group of educators with a collective vision to create a cultural and educational center for families. NCCM started as a Museums Without Walls that traveled weekly to bookstores, bakeries, and community centers throughout the region. These pop-up exhibits and workshops offered interactive programs for children 12 and under and their families in a wide range of STEAM (Science, Technology, Engineering, Arts, Math) topics.

Watching an idea grow has been an incredibly rewarding experience for the staff and many volunteers who have worked to make the museum a reality. It is a great joy to share NCCM – and the wonders of learning something new—with your family!

Adirondack for Kids

Kids Matter Most

Adirondack for Kids is a fund started by the Adirondack Family of Businesses to offer grants to nonprofit organizations supporting youth activities in the Communities where we work, live, and play.

(518) 483-3835 • www.AdirondackEnergy.com/Adirondack-for-kids

BIG SPOON
— KITCHEN —

Big Spoon Kitchen's mission is to connect people with the wonderful local food resources we have right here in our community.

WEEKLY MENU
- A changing weekly menu goes up Thursday morning on our website
- Order until Monday morning
- Pick-up is Tues. 3-6 in Potsdam or there is a Wednesday delivery option
- Freezer items are always available
- Using local vegetables, fruits, meats, eggs, and sweeteners

CLASSES
Learn a kitchen skill by scheduling a class. Basic knife skills, empanadas, pizza making, and more. No secret recipes at Big Spoon!

CATERING
Let us handle the food at your next event! Call us to discuss menu options.

CONTACT US
bigspoonpotsdam.com

315-244-8888

bigspoonpotsdam@gmail.com

6510 NY-56   Potsdam NY, 13676   315-244-8888

bigspoonpotsdam@gmail.com

www.bigspoonpotsdam.com

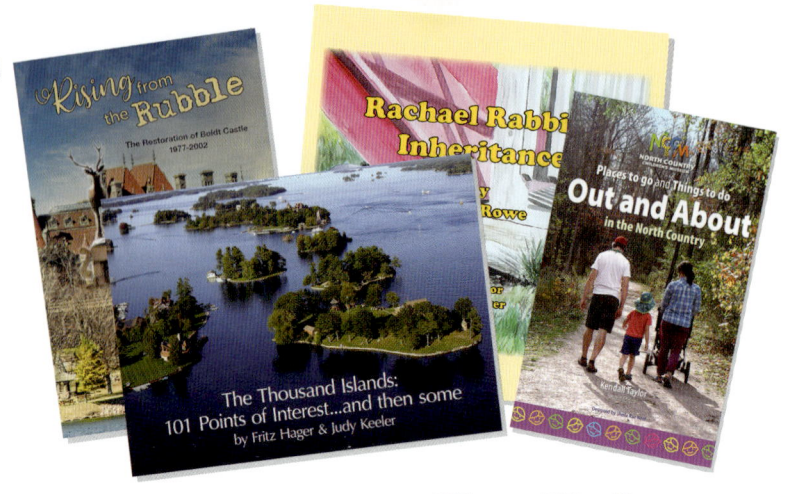

coughlin
coughlin.co

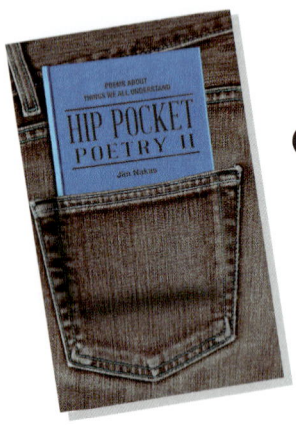

offering
Custom Book Printing
short run digital
or
bulk offset quantities

in 2 locations:

210 Court Street, Suite 10
Watertown, NY 13601
315-788-8560

7602 N State Street
Lowville, NY 13367
315-376-3224

coughlin
coughlin.co

WE'RE YOUR COMMUNITY PARTNERS FOR LIFE

For more than 85 years, we've been a family in business, making a positive difference in people's lives.

We're proud to be caring citizens and to partner with organizations like the **North Country Children's Museum**, helping them to enhance and improve the quality of life in the neighborhoods where we live and work.

Price Chopper®

www.pricechopper.com

We're not just in your neighborhood, we're your neighbor.

Please consider a gift to the Potsdam Holiday Fund so that we can help to make the holidays a little brighter for local children in need.

The Potsdam Holiday Fund serves families in Potsdam, Madrid, Hopkinton, Nicholville, Brasher Falls, Chase Mills, Fort Jackson, West Stockholm and Winthrop.

Gifts are accepted and appreciated year-round at potsdamholidayfund.org.

The Potsdam Holiday Fund Inc. is a 501(c)(3) organization. Contributions to the fund are tax deductible as allowed by the IRS.

(This ad paid for by friends of the Potsdam Holiday Fund.)

Future-Focused Fun!
DISCOVER CLARKSON

*All photos are pre-COVID

clarkson.edu

fth CABINETRY

Free Estimate & Design

Visit our showroom
6 Pioneer Drive, Potsdam

315.268.0713

fthcabinetry.com
Find us on Facebook, Instagram, Flickr

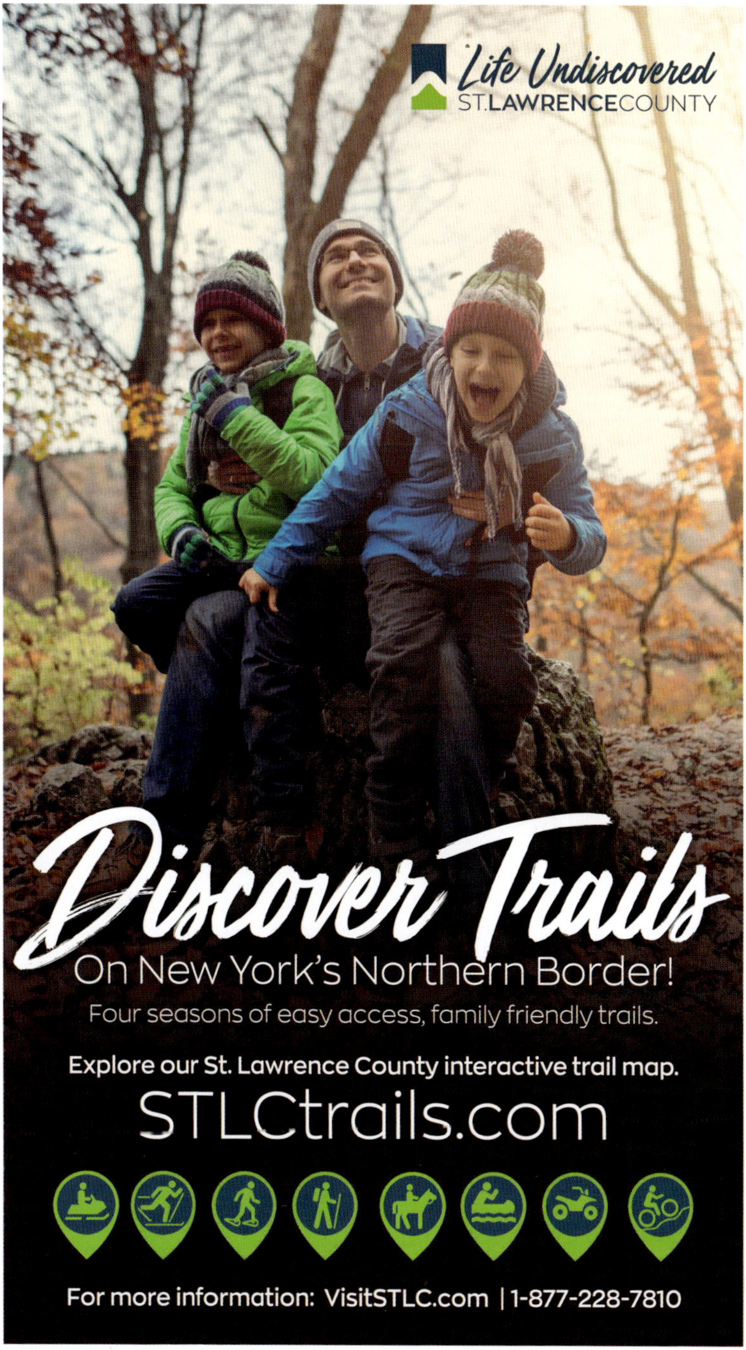
Life Undiscovered
ST.LAWRENCECOUNTY
Discover Trails
On New York's Northern Border!
Four seasons of easy access, family friendly trails.
Explore our St. Lawrence County interactive trail map.
STLCtrails.com
For more information: VisitSTLC.com | 1-877-228-7810

Decades of Experience in North Country Real Estate

NIKKI COATES & ASSOCIATES

Licensed Real Estate Broker

30 Main Street
Potsdam, NY 13676
315 – 265 – 4303

LOCAL FOODS AND BREWS

Raise a Glass Inside
...or on the Deck

Lunch: 11:30 am - 4 pm
Dinner: 5 - 8 pm
Sunday Brunch: 10 am - 3 pm
Closed Tuesdays

Reservations Suggested

Weekly Signature
COCKTAILS

Innovative, Contemporary
LOCAL CUISINE

Good Things Happen at Jake's

5726 SH 56 • Hannawa Falls • 315-274-9300
www.jakesonthewater.com

Jake's
Lunch ❧ Dinner ❧ Cocktails

KinneyDrugs

Employee-owned.
Locally committed.
Since 1903.

www.KinneyDrugs.com